EPIDEMIC OF LIFE

Epidemic of Life

*Becoming a Contagious Christian to
Reach a Desperate World*

CHRIS THACKERY

WORD PUBLISHING
Milton Keynes, England

EPIDEMIC OF LIFE

First edition published 2000 by Word Publishing,
9 Holdom Avenue, Bletchley, Milton Keynes, Bucks, MK1 1QR, UK.

ISBN 1 86024 358 4

Designed and produced for Word Publishing by
Bookprint Creative Services, P.O. Box 827, BN21 3YJ, England.
Printed in Great Britain.

DEDICATION

To all my families, especially to my wife
Charlotte, and my wonderful
children.

ACKNOWLEDGMENTS

I wish to express my heartfelt thanks to all those who, sometimes unwittingly, have helped to shape this book: to Malcolm Down for his support and encouragement, and the willingness to take on an untried author; to Jane Hamilton for all her editorial work, mostly against tight deadlines; to my church, who have with cheerful longsuffering acted as the guinea pigs for developing many of the ideas contained in this book; and above all to my wife, Charlotte, without whose support this book would not have progressed beyond piles of paper and good intentions.

CONTENTS

FOREWORD

It is a great pleasure to be able to write a foreword to *Epidemic of Life*.

I have read a number of books recently that look critically and analytically at the Church today, calling for a rethink in many key areas. "What is the purpose and nature of Church? How are we going to evangelise in a rapidly-changing society? How do we make disciples in a post-modern culture?"

These are extremely important questions.

But many of the books that I have read have not, in fact, given answers and indeed reflect a measure of disillusionment and pain. In this book, Chris Thackery not only raises the critical questions and the brave questions but you will also find practical and dynamic answers. Answers that come out of hard-won experience seeking to build Church in a particularly tough area of London.

I appreciate Chris' forthright thinking, the strong challenges he brings to our priorities and attitudes, and his hands-on approach to some of the big challenges that face the Church today.

Whether you agree with the contents of this book or not is immaterial, but read it! It is a must for any of us who are seeking to be relevant in a post-modern environment, who are seeking to tackle the big issues.

This book is very necessary reading. I wholeheartedly support it and encourage it.

Laurence Singlehurst
UK Director of YWAM

Prologue

EPIDEMIC OF LIFE

And the Lord added to their number daily those who were being saved (Acts 2:47).

The early Church spread like an epidemic. Within a few decades of Jesus' death and resurrection, the Gospel had reached most of the known world. Groups of Jesus' followers, known simply as The Way, were springing up everywhere. These groups were remarkable: they comprised both men and women worshipping together as equals, a revolution at the time; they were converts from right across the spiritual and intellectual spectrum: paganism, Judaism, cult worshippers, philosophers. They were found in both urban and rural areas. They included people of high social rank, and the poorest of the poor; people from every walk of life, from many ethnic groups, of all levels of ability and every different personality type. Their beliefs were challenging, but more than that, these beliefs had brought about a transformation in personal lifestyle and behaviour that was visible, recognisable, maybe a little scary, but deeply attractive. And in their relationships with each other, in those communities of love, outsiders saw something that undeniably had life, joy, and a freedom that was profoundly, achingly enviable.

In short, they were radically contagious . . .

Part I

ANOTHER DIMENSION

Chapter 1

THE CHALLENGE

How's business? Is what we're doing effective? Are we working to our full potential? These are questions we need to ask. Our business is, after all, the most important on earth: bringing God's love to a desperate world.

Taking ground

After a century of decline, recent years have brought many signs of encouragement to the UK church. We have seen a new openness to the work of the Holy Spirit, especially in charismatic gifts; we've seen new styles of worship, a new freedom in the form and content of church meetings. Although still the subject of debate, we've learned much about the apostolic and prophetic ministries referred to in Ephesians 4. There has been a growing emphasis on church as a body, with all its members taking part, breaking down the traditional gap between clergy and laity. There has been a growth of confidence, reflected in innovative work amongst young people and a willingness to grapple with modern culture and sub-cultures. We have also seen a great deal of investment from overseas, such as the teaching of John Wimber and missions by Billy Graham and Luis Palau. In the nineties we've seen the impact of the 'Toronto blessing' and the Pensacola revival. Bible weeks have mush-roomed, training courses have multiplied; some churches have become 'seeker sensitive', some have developed church planting strategies, others have adopted cell structures, and large numbers are running Alpha courses. Many church leaders are testifying to a progressive lowering of denominational barriers, and to new opportunities to work together with other churches in their area.

The job still to be done

Despite this encouragement, there is clearly much still to be done:

Breakthrough. For all that the huge crowds at Bible weeks are impressive, the fact remains that Christians are still only a tiny proportion of the population. The combined attendance at Spring Harvest and Stoneleigh Bible weeks only matches the crowd that Manchester United draws for every home game. To the vast majority of people we are largely invisible and of marginal relevance.

Ethnic minorities. The briefest of surveys at Christian events would confirm a heavy preponderance of ethnic white people. There is of course a significant black Pentecostal presence, but by and large very little from other ethnic groups, with especially poor representation from Asian peoples.

Working class and underclass. At the risk of generalising, charismatic evangelicalism in particular seems to be particularly strong in the suburban middle classes, and considerably weaker in urban areas, especially in the working class and underclass.

Men. In the majority of UK churches, women significantly outnumber men.

The challenge of change

While these issues alone give us good reason for sober reflection, there are other points to consider.

Society in transition: post modernism

Change is here to stay, and it's proving hard to live with. People are facing isolation due to the breakdown of community, the pressures of urban life, the changes in gender roles, economic uncertainty and moral confusion. Dissatisfaction with life, even desperation, is mirrored in the explosion of interest in self-help and counselling, and in a spiralling suicide rate. There's a sea of change taking place as our society shifts from a modernist worldview into post-modernism. It's not easy to get a handle on post-modernism: it isn't a system or a philosophy as such, more a set of values that are permeating through our society. The following are some of the core values:

- There is a deep distrust of institutions and authority, which are seen as oppressive to the individual.
- Truth is relative, there are no absolutes: what's true for you may not be true for me.
- There are likewise no absolutes in ethical behaviour. If a certain behaviour is generally accepted then it's OK.
- There are no 'big answers': ideologies are seen as an imposition, intruding on the rights of individuals to decide how they should live.
- Cultural values can be mixed and matched from a market place of ideas and beliefs to provide a blend that suits the individual.
- Spirituality is acceptable, (much more so than to the modernist mind-set), but is seen as strictly personal and private.

Essentially, post-modern man seeks to shape morals, values and spirituality to suit himself.

It would be difficult to overstate the challenge this presents.

The Church, of course, is not only perceived by many people as an institution (and they're probably more right than we'd like to admit!) but as one that claims authority of the sort that post modernists find intolerable. The belief that there are absolutes of truth and morality, that there is a 'big answer', that spiritual truth is universal, corporate and public, are all central to the Christian message.

Like it or not, we're becoming counter-cultural at a rate that's way beyond comfortable.

Society in transition: the post-Christian age

Since the conversion of Constantine, and the declaration of Christianity as the officially recognised religion of the Roman Empire, the Church, which began as a radical movement outside governmental and existing social structures, became inextricably intertwined with the state. Church leaders acquired political power, became agents of government. Church structures became central to social organisation, judicial systems and education. Church doctrines not only defined the spiritual values of society but even determined the framework for morality, science and the arts. Christian values provided the baseline, however badly understood or complied with. This whole edifice, Christendom, has been under pressure for quite some time, but shows signs of crumbling much more rapidly in this century. In a globalised, multi-racial society Christian values are no longer accepted as the default.

This has major implications. On the down side, we are already witnessing the destructive effects on our society as it progressively deviates from biblical principles of healthy living. This seems likely to get worse before it improves. On the positive side, an emerging population that is largely ignorant of Christianity may prove easier to evangelise than one that is subject to misconception and negative associations. And perhaps the church has a new opportunity to develop an identity that is clearly distinct from the establishment. It has an opportunity to become a radical counter-culture of the first century model.

Responses

Given these challenges, in what direction should we look for answers?

Tuning in to the culture. Much work in recent years has been invested in helping the Church to become more culturally relevant. The basic idea has been to communicate the Gospel in ways that are credible to the target audience, both by trying to understand the issues of concern to the target group and adopting an appropriate style of presentation. The results have been highly innovative, creative, sometimes controversial, often fruitful and very occasionally disastrous. While there is a great deal of merit in following this path, will this provide the type of breakthrough that we need? I have doubts on several grounds.

In the past, a person's primary sense of belonging was provided by their family, their community and their workplace, often with a considerable overlap of all three. Now, this sense of belonging and identity is expressed in a bewildering variety of different people-groups gathered around shared interests, beliefs, music, sports, political views, even medical conditions. People may belong to a number of such cultures, each quite distinct. Youth sub-cultures in particular seem especially prone to rapid change and fragmentation. Youth sub-cultures can also be particularly demanding of conformity to their current values: presentations of the Gospel that are not bang up to date are immediately scorned. And of course in most urban areas there is the need to recognise the cultural implications of a multi-racial society.

The danger is that we could be drawn into a massive effort of cultural adaptation to reach an ever increasing number of people-groups on their own terms, only to find that many of them have evolved further leaving us forever playing 'catch-up'.

And there is the risk that the focus of our thinking shifts to
'culture' instead of the issues that individual people face. Let
me put it in crude terms: my experience is that all my reading
and wrestling with the issues of post-modernism have done
little to increase my effectiveness when faced, for example, with
a young woman who has spent the housekeeping on the lottery
and is terrified of facing her violent boyfriend when he comes
home.

It's easy to lose sight of individual people. We can talk in
terms of culture and sub-culture, and devise strategies and programs and initiatives to reach them, finding structural solutions
to structural problems. In doing so, I fear that we may be
missing the obvious, which is that in the end, within the structures are people, individuals with a need, whether they know it
or not, for God. We can become so intent on the differences
between all the sub-cultures, that we can overlook the fact that
all human beings have, deep down, the same needs. Perhaps if
we as Christians focussed on touching people at these levels, we
would be more fruitful, even across cultural divides.

New Testament Christians undoubtedly accepted the need to
recognise cultural differences: Paul talks of being a Jew to the
Jews, a Gentile to the Gentiles, and uses local poets as a starting point for one of his sermons. And yet at the same time one
is struck by the fact that the majority of instruction in the New
Testament is directed towards personal transformation and
guidance for godly relationships. There is very little teaching on
culturally relevant evangelism. Indeed, the volume of instruction on any form of evangelism is really quite small. Could this
be because a transformed people, expressing a new form of
community were inherently, contagiously evangelistic?

Changing Church structures. As I described above, there have
been many exciting changes in our churches over the last twenty
years. It's interesting to note how many of these focus on
church structures, and church corporate activities. There is an

almost ceaseless procession of new ways of 'doing church', whether new ways of organising or new programs. Could this be the way forward? Can we see radical breakthroughs by getting the right combination and style of meetings? Or will the next initiative be the decisive one?

The New Testament gives scant attention to church structures and organisation. There are some references of course: the appointment of the seven to organise food distribution in Acts 6, and the appointing of elders spring to mind. Yet even here the instructions regarding elders and deacons are not primarily organisational: rather they define their character qualifications.

It's sobering to think that even for our more committed church members, regularly attending perhaps a Sunday meeting, and a mid-week group of some sort, the time spent in these activities is probably less than 5% of their waking week. Yet fine-tuning and re-organising these activities can occupy a very large slice of the time and efforts of everyone, especially Church leaders. If we're honest, most of us would admit that while the 5% is valuable in itself, it has far too little impact on the 95% of our lives which takes place outside church meetings. Too often our church activities fail to equip us for the rest of our life. The secular/spiritual divide remains, with our spiritual life still trying to fight its way out of a corner, and we find it hard to live lives that are very much distinct from the lives of not-yet-Christians around us.

A different dimension. In the Bible the men of Issachar are commended for 'understanding the times', and I firmly believe in the importance of Christians grappling with contemporary culture. Likewise, I consider it vital that we work constantly to make our Church structures effective, streamlined and flexible. But we shouldn't expect more of structures than they can deliver.

I'm convinced that we need to think in a different dimension, a dimension that focuses on change within people. It's good that we have seen twenty years of church reforms and initiatives, yet there's a sense that they've been bolted on to something that has remained largely untouched. They're like jewels looking for a crown. I think we need a fresh vision: to help congregations of people become those crowns! We need now to fill our *reformed* churches with *transformed* people. It is good to have *effective* church structures. But now we need to make sure our *effective* Churches are full of *contagious* Christians.

This is not a new idea: in fact it's central to the New Testament. The New Testament doesn't talk about churchgoers; or people who go to meetings; in fact even the word 'Christian' only occurs three times. Rather it talks about 'disciples' (289 references). The word 'disciple' means a pupil, a follower, an adherent, one who imitates his master. But the New Testament adds an incredible dimension to this: disciples are those who are being 'transformed into His likeness with ever increasing glory' (2 Cor 3:18). This is an awesome idea. A people who are becoming like Jesus Christ himself will be filling up with a life that permeates, illuminates and changes every aspect of their lives. This life that brings joy and truth and freedom, works at the very depths of our humanity, transforming those elements that are common to all people. It has the capacity to spread like an epidemic. A people living in this dimension breaks out of cultural niches and has an impact across the divides of age, class, gender, culture, ethnic origin, and background. People who are living like Him will expose injustice, challenge lies, and turn the world upside down by love. Just like Jesus did. That's all Jesus has ever wanted: people like Himself. He wants *strong churches* full of *dangerous disciples*.

Is this possible? I believe that the answer is resoundingly 'Yes!' The US army has as its recruiting slogan: 'Be all that you can be'. And that's the purpose behind this book, to sow a fresh vision of what we can be as followers of the Way. But a slogan is meaningless by itself and visions too are empty unless they are 'earthed' to reality. The US army has to put its recruits through a great deal of training to realise the goal.

My aim is to propose principles and practical ideas to help us realise the goals of true discipleship.

But first, a key question: Given the New Testament vision of true discipleship, and the priority it's accorded, why in our churches is such awesome potential so significantly unrealised? This calls us to a hard look at our theology. And I suspect that we've been looking aslant for some time . . .

SUMMARY

There has been much from which to draw encouragement in our churches over the last twenty years. But there is much still to do: we have yet to see the decisive breakthrough in numbers, and we have still to overcome significant barriers of class, location, race and gender. Further challenges are presented by our society's transition into post-modernism and the post-Christian age. Learning to adapt to our culture is valuable; reforming our churches is necessary, but in addition we need to look at a different dimension, filling our churches with people being transformed into the likeness of Christ. One purpose of this book is to refresh the vision of what we're called to be as disciples. The other goal is to put forward some practical tools that may help us to be radical followers of Jesus, followers of the Way, Christians who are becoming truly fulfilled and dangerously contagious. We are to be God's epidemic of life to the world.

Chapter 2

FIRING ON ALL CYLINDERS
THE THEOLOGY OF CONTAGIOUS
CHRISTIANITY

The Cross and the empty tomb: restoring the balance

The Western Church has for centuries regarded the Cross as the centrepiece of Christian doctrine, and seen salvation primarily in terms of the forgiveness of sins. This is so familiar to us that it comes as something of a surprise to find that the early Christians had a different perspective. The early Christians certainly preached the Cross, but they equally emphasised the Resurrection: 'Christ is risen' was their glorious news, the proof that the life that Jesus himself had, and the life to the full that he promised to his followers, was real and powerful enough to conquer death! If we look at Jesus' own teaching then certainly we see the themes of repentance, reconciliation and ransom woven throughout. But we also see that in fact a greater proportion of His teaching focuses on the Kingdom, and on true life. The coming Kingdom is a repeated theme, and a large number of His parables communicate the nature of this Kingdom and how to enter it. He taught about the necessity for newness of life; His Sermon on the Mount describes how this life is to be lived, and central to His message is the declaration that in Him is abundant life: 'I have come that they may have life, and have it to the full' (John 10:10). It's a life of true freedom, a life that is so powerful that it gushes like streams from within, empowers us to reign over our present circumstances and lasts for eternity.

The pre-occupation of the Western Church with salvation in terms of forgiveness of sins emerged some centuries later. This happened at a time when much of the life-spark of the early Christians had dimmed, when the Church had transformed from a radical persecuted sect into the official religion of the Roman Empire. It is interesting to note in passing that even the use of the Cross as a symbol in Christian art didn't emerge until well into the 5th Century.

I want to be clear on this point: I am certainly not saying that our theology is in itself wrong, but I do think that it is significantly out of balance. This imbalance has some serious implications that we need to face up to.

Evangelistic problem. If we see the Gospel message primarily in terms of being saved from our sins, we have a significant evangelistic problem in that our post-Christian and post-modern society has a very poor awareness of its sinfulness. We are in danger of preaching a solution to people who don't even acknowledge that the problem really exists. It's not surprising that for many people our message seems to be of limited relevance.

Saved from – Saved for. Our theology is in sharp focus when it comes to the event of salvation; we are clear about repentance, Jesus' vicarious death, our forgiveness and reconciliation: in short, making converts. But the picture is considerably more blurry and indistinct on the business of living out this new life we've received, living as a disciple. We have a theology that is strong on what we are saved from, but much weaker on what we are saved for. Many Christians can tell me four steps I need to take to be saved from my sins and born again. Considerably fewer can tell me so clearly just what I'm saved for, still less how to do it. We see so many Christians whose early growth has reached a plateau, whose new life has calcified into routine. Although few would admit it rationally, there's an underlying thought that if I'm saved and going to heaven, what need is there for anything else? Where there's no real vision of the purpose of discipleship, living out New Testament principles can quickly decay into a legalistic chore. Even where people have a vision to grow, our theology of discipleship usually fails to give the practical tools that are necessary to pursue it.

Human-centred. A third problem is that presenting the Gospel so heavily weighted towards the forgiveness of sins creates a gravitational pull towards a human-centred perspective. God's primary purpose becomes the rescue of humanity from the Fall. Self-centredness is, of course, a disease endemic to sinful man, but sadly our theology has proved too accommodating. We have churches full of people who respond to God as though His primary purpose is to solve their problems, make them feel better, and who continue to live in the 'I' centred world of their old nature.

Reaching men. Finally, the fact that the message is so heavily weighted towards restored relationship with a loving God through the forgiveness of sins, may explain why it seems to be so much less attractive to men than women. A Gospel that emphasises life to the full, tackles the practical challenges of living a radical lifestyle, and with a sharper sense of purpose may prove altogether more engaging.

In short, we need to take a fresh look at what we understand by the Gospel. We need to add a far greater emphasis on what we're saved for, on abundant life and on discipleship. I have no wish, in any way, to undermine the cosmic significance of the Cross, or the profound importance of the forgiveness of sins, and reconciliation to our Father in heaven. But I am saying that the Gospel as portrayed *in the Bible* is bigger than the one we have been preaching. We need to *add* these dimensions to our message. I do not wish to downplay anything we currently communicate. Rather my hope is that by seeing the bigger picture, we will find ourselves with a healthier balance and a message that is more faithful, relevant, attractive, and contagious. What does this message look like?

Life to the full

God is wild and free! Our Gospel message must begin not with mankind, nor with the Fall, but with God Himself, and with His purposes even before the creation of the world. The Bible says that God is happy![1] Twice in the New Testament he is called 'blessed' (1 Tim 1:11, 1 Tim 6:15), and He acts according to His good pleasure. He lives in His own glory and He celebrates Himself. God is wild and free. The Father's desire is to glorify the Son (Phil 2:9), the Son glorifies the Father (John 13:31–32) and the Holy Spirit glorifies the Son (John 16:14). This is the awesome relationship of the Trinity. God created the world, and humanity, for His glory (Ps 19:1; Is 43:7). God's purpose in creating human beings was to extend His family, to have children, co-heirs with Christ (Eph 1:5). Before the creation of the world we were chosen to be holy (Eph 1:4), predestined to be like Jesus, to be glorified (Rom 8:29–30), to be one with Him, joining in that wonderful celebration of joy and love, completely fulfilled. When Adam and Eve were created they were designed to live in this joyous intimate relationship with God. They were called to multiply: God gave them the awesome privilege of being involved in His plans to fill the earth with His family! He also called them to rule the earth, giving them, like himself, a purpose, and giving them authority under His own authority (Genesis 1:28). This is the glorious life we were designed for: joyous intimacy with God; purpose; and connected into the mains power supply: drawing life and the power to live directly from the Source Himself.

Our destination[2]. The Book of Revelation shows us where God's plans lead: we see our destination there. We will see Him face to face, we will reign with Him, celebrate with Him, glorify Him and be glorified by Him. We will be full of eternal life, living in a city which shines with the glory of God, where there is perfect peace, fulfilment, excitement, truth, justice, plenty of all we need, laughter, a wedding feast.

Running on batteries. But something went wrong: Adam and Eve chose to rebel against God; the Fall took place. They decided to glorify themselves, to be independent of God. They became selfish, self-centred, doing things that dishonoured God, a pattern followed by every human being since. People and creation are not designed for this, and so we see a mess. Human beings, cut off from the mains supply of life, are running on batteries. These run out. Death. Some people are trying to get back to God through philosophy, good deeds and religion: to no avail. Some people are desperate for purpose and fulfilment and they pursue power, money, status. Futile. Others desperately seek love and follow one disastrous relationship with another. Others are simply running from the pain, taking refuge in drugs, crime and alcohol. Nothing works.

Message of life! What humanity cannot do, God did! Jesus came into the world bringing a message of hope: new birth to a new life, life to the full, living in the kingdom of God! He demonstrated the fullness of this life for which we are designed. It's a life that has as its object the glory of God, a life that is connected to God, and flows with love, power, peace, authority, healing, and joy. He died on the Cross to cancel out everything in us that dishonours God. Then He rose from the dead and ascended to the Father, demonstrating that His life is more powerful than death. Partaking of His life, we have both life to

the full and life that goes on forever! Jesus is the ␣ ␣ ␣
death to life!

Into His likeness. Now everyone on the planet has a ch␣ ␣ ␣␣␣
carry on with battery power until the battery runs out, or to
cross the bridge and get back on track with God's purposes for
us, to enter into all that we're designed for. When we choose to
go over that bridge, the power of our old sinful nature is
broken; it was crucified on the Cross. Once over the bridge, our
new life has just begun. Our purpose is to glorify God in everything we do. But we have been damaged and scarred by our
experiences in a fallen world; we have acquired bad habits of
thought, word and behaviour. To realise the fullness of life
given to us, we work together with God to break free of the
dead but restrictive cocoon of our old life, and to nurture the
growth of our new life up to full stature. This is the process of
discipleship: working with God to be transformed into His likeness. Central to this 'likeness' is that we are only truly fulfilled
when we live utterly for God rather than for ourselves. We truly
live when we truly love; we truly love when we sacrifice. Jesus
demonstrated this by His complete submission to the Father;
and on the Cross. He taught us that the principle for life is the
principle of the Cross: 'whoever loses his life for me will find it'
(Luke 9:24).

Investing in eternity. As disciples, we have a new identity; we are
children of God, increasingly like Him. But this also has profound implications for what we do. As people of the Kingdom
of God, living according to the will of God, our every action
has awesome new potential. Jesus says that godly deeds store up
treasure in heaven (Mark 10:21). Paul explains to the
Corinthians that all our works will be tested, and that which is
built of gold will endure (1 Cor 3:12–15). When the earth is
purified by fire, and we enter the new heavens and earth, incredibly we will see there some of our handiwork: all those words

and thoughts that honour God, those of our deeds obedient to His will. God has given us the amazing privilege of sharing in the creation of our eternal home! As disciples we are dealing *every* moment with choices that have an eternal dimension. There is no neutral ground: we are either building things which will endure, or things that will not. And this isn't just about our 'spiritual' activities: it applies equally to those times given to the daily routines of living, which can be lived either in communion with God, or emptily.

Jesus' instruction in the Great Commission to teach disciples to obey is there, not because God wants to exert control over us. It's about God's desire to restore us to our original purpose; His intention to call us to share in His work of creation and partake of His divine nature (2 Pet 1:4).

And our participation in His purposes is not restricted to ourselves as individuals; it is corporate too. We are born into a family, the Church, whose purpose is to preach the Gospel to the ends of the earth and declare the wisdom of God in the heavenly realms (Eph 3:10). We are God's fellow workers as His Kingdom of truth, justice and righteousness advances forcefully, ultimately engulfing everything tainted by the Fall. Death in all its forms is swallowed up in life!

The heart of discipleship

When our perspective of the Gospel is brought into balance like this, it has huge implications for our understanding of discipleship and may call us to make a number of key paradigm shifts:

Means and ends. Viewed from this angle, we can see that living as a disciple is about becoming more like Jesus, living to glorify God in everything we do; and that in so living we will be perfectly fulfilled. This perspective emphasises that our conversion is not the end but the *beginning* of the most exciting journey! You can't be a disciple without being a convert, but to be a convert and not a disciple means that you're missing out on the very purpose for which you were saved. You've mistaken the means for the end. Perhaps even our use of the term 'Christian' to describe ourselves is somewhat unfortunate: it has the effect of emphasising what we have become, whereas the word disciple, used far more extensively in the New Testament carries more of a sense of 'becoming'. We are disciples *of* someone, we are following after Him, becoming like Him, our hero and role model.

Every aspect of life. The New Testament shows us that growing as a disciple, learning to live life to the full, affects every aspect of our lives: our thoughts, our words, our priorities; our relationships with our spouse, our children, our work colleagues, our enemies, and our fellow disciples. It has an impact on the way we handle money; the way we make decisions; they way we eat; the way we work; the way we rest; our approach to sex; our hopes for the future; our purpose for living; our attitude to ourselves. We have a new life, not simply some spiritual accessories to our old life. Our new life touches our television habits, our alcohol problem, what we say about relatives, our reaction to the taxman, and so on. When we see this life emerging in us we become excited. We want to tell people; we become contagious! When others see the changes in us, see us living life more abundantly, they are drawn, even across cultural barriers. They become more open to receive the truth, because they've already seen it in action.

Good news as well as good history. It is revealing that for so many Christians, the very words 'giving testimony' are synonymous with 'explaining how I came to be converted'. Most of us have that off pat. But if we stopped our church members in the street and asked them how they had changed and grown in the last month, what answers would we get? As we restore the balance of our theology, we also restore the balance of our testimony to not-yet-Christians. Our message is not only 'what God did' however many years ago, but 'what God is doing now'; we balance the testimony of conversion with the testimony of discipleship, the living proof that God is at work right now! What we communicate will constantly be updated as we see God work within us: our message becomes good news as well as good history.

A practical business. This process of 'taking hold of that for which Christ Jesus laid hold of me' (Phil 3:12) is an immensely practical business. It involves working out more clearly what life to the full actually looks like and how it works; in a sense we need to reshape every facet of our lives. It means discovering which of our values, behaviours, attitudes and thoughts belong to the old nature and therefore require demolition. It means learning how to live in communion with God. It means learning about and applying the tools that God gives for putting off the old nature, and putting on the new. These are often specific actions, applied with discipline, accountability and perseverance, through the power of the Holy Spirit.

Understanding of Scripture. A significant proportion of the New Testament is given over to instructions and commands. I once went through and listed them all, filling ten pages of closely printed A4 paper. Without a strong and clear theology of discipleship we can easily become confused. We all know that sometimes there can be one theology in our minds, but a quite different one in our hearts! In our minds we may know well enough that we're saved by grace and not by works. But faced with the extent of these instructions and commands many Christians are living as though keeping them is the due payback for salvation, or is necessary to earn God's favour, or to maintain their salvation. In a fallen world, wherever we leave even a partial truth vacuum, legalism is one of the first errors to fill the space.

But when we have a healthy theology of discipleship, all this can be transformed. The instructions and commands in the New Testament are seen in their true light: not as a set of rules, legalistic handcuffs, but as a guide to living life to the full! They describe what life to the full looks like, how to enter into it, how to come into the joy, fulfilment and freedom of Jesus himself! In this light obedience is not a sombre duty to appease an exacting deity. Rather it's a joyful expression of the true life our loving Father is nurturing within us.

A new motivation. When discipleship is seen merely as some form of optional add-on to being born again, then the motivation for living biblically is hard to sustain. Alternatively, for many Christians the call to obedience is seen as the small print of salvation, something that we ought to do as a form of payback in response to His kindness in saving us. Similarly, if our motivation is based on this, on obligation and debt-paying, we will quickly find ourselves flagging. The result, either way, is Christians living lives that are often hard to distinguish from the lives of not-yet-Christians, constantly on the defensive, trying not to sin but regularly overwhelmed by their old nature. Growth is slow. But when we see discipleship's true purpose, when we cultivate our vision of the fullness of life that comes from living God's way, a crucial change takes place: instead of 'trying not to sin' we find that we no longer *want* to sin, because we see clearly its cost to us, the damage it does. Our motivation to holiness is engaged, and growth is much more rapid.

Agenda. Two directions emerge from all of this. Firstly, the evangelistic. It is vital that we adjust the way we communicate the Gospel to reflect these points. This will make our Gospel more biblical, more intelligible, more credible and more attractive. If new believers being added to our churches understood the call to discipleship from the outset, if their conversion represented not only a desire for forgiveness and a fresh start but a passion to become like Jesus, how church life would be transformed! My suggestions on how we might present this approach to the Gospel to our unsaved friends are in the Appendix, not reflecting any lesser importance, but because the primary thrust of this present book lies more towards the transformation of those who are already Christians.

This is the second direction. Having outlined a theology, how can we work it out in practice? How can we get a handle on the paradigm shifts? How are we transformed into His likeness?

SUMMARY

The Western Church has a Gospel message that is heavily weighted towards the Crucifixion and the forgiveness of sins. This emphasis may prove increasingly difficult to communicate in a post-modern, post-Christian society. It carries more danger of becoming man-centred, and has a weak theology of discipleship. Restoring the balance of our message, beginning with God and His ultimate purposes, and emphasising life to the full, what we're saved *for*, opens the door to an understanding of discipleship which is more coherent and immensely exciting! It sows the vision for a process of transformation touching every aspect of life.

Part II

INTO HIS LIKENESS

Chapter 3

HOW CHANGE WORKS

God's idea of discipleship is people being transformed into the likeness of Christ. In becoming more like Jesus, His disciples are increasingly living life to the full. This life to the full touches every aspect of existence, from the most exalted to the most mundane, and energises it, beautifies it, fills it with light. Disciples so transformed are contagious; people without that light see it and thirst for it. Disciples so transformed are dangerous, bringing the Kingdom of God against everything contrary to God.

But *how* do we change? And how do we *stay* changed? We've all had 'life-changing' spiritual experiences, only to find ourselves reverting to old ways a few weeks later. How can we hold our gains? Let's lay the foundation stone first, the basic principle of transformation: our partnership with the Holy Spirit.

The pull of legalism

How do we change? At one end of the scale we have the view that inner transformation, the process of sanctification, is a matter of compliance with New Testament instructions through a structured regime of rules, principles and patterns. But we've probably all seen instances where this approach has decayed into an empty legalism. After a while the 'quiet time' becomes an arid routine, life becomes progressively narrower, constrained by *don't*, *ought*, *should* and *must*. Relying on one's own power is insufficient to bring real change. A legalistic Christian faces repeated failure leading to discouragement, guilt and shame. When we live by a set of rules we cannot fulfil, we find before long that our perspective of God as our loving Father is replaced by an image of a stern father who is disappointed, and can never be pleased. And then we find ourselves seeking to earn His favour by our actions. This may be subconscious, but nevertheless we are no longer, in truth, living the Gospel. The Apostle Paul's repeated challenges to legalism, especially in the letter to the Galatians, show how pervasive and dangerous it is. In fact, legalism seems to be one of the primary defaults of fallen humanity.

Let go and let God?

The charismatic movement has seen something of a swing to the other extreme partly as a reaction to the stifling, leaden weight of legalism. The 'let go and let God' philosophy enshrined even on our fridge magnets and car stickers, declares that we are completely dependent on the Holy Spirit, that He alone can change us. So far, so good. But problems creep in when we start to believe that we ourselves have no part to play in this process. We can quickly find ourselves opting out of our responsibility, adopting a fatalistic attitude, tolerating sin on the basis that we're waiting for God to deal with it. We can find ourselves living for the quick fix, waiting for the power encounter that will solve each of our problems. We become super-spiritual: we may have a façade that looks so worthy, yet in truth we've become self-centred and passive. The result is that we remain superficial and immature. Opting out of responsibility is another of fallen humanity's primary defaults.

Working in partnership

The biblical pattern for inward change is not the drudge of responsibility without power that we see in legalism; neither is it the superficiality of seeking power without exercising responsibility. It lies in working together with the Holy Spirit, a partnership with God himself!

Living by grace. The Scriptures are clear and specific: God indwells his children (Col 1:27). His power is at work in us. We cannot live life to the full and we cannot be transformed by our own limited resources. Battery power simply isn't enough: we have to be connected to the mains supply. We are not only saved by grace but are to live by grace. This is a crucial concept. I suspect that many of us need to re-think our understanding of grace. Most Christians primarily associate grace with justification: we're saved by grace not by works (Eph 2:8–9). But generally speaking our understanding of grace to live is much fuzzier: we may wish each other 'the grace of our Lord Jesus Christ' but do we really know what it means? I think the formulas we use to shed light on grace actually cast more shadows: defining grace as 'God's unmerited favour' simply won't suffice. There are several references to the Father's grace resting on Jesus (Luke 2:40) and it would be hard to argue anything other than that this favour was supremely merited! Likewise the acrostic '**G**od's **R**iches **A**t **C**hrist's **E**xpense' is helpful to a point but still too narrow, and portrays grace as too static. Throughout the New Testament, Paul constantly refers to the grace that gave him his calling to the Gentiles (Eph 3:7–8), the grace that was the source of his holiness and sincerity (2 Cor 1:12), the grace which equipped him for his ministry ((2 Cor 12:9). Our definition of grace must expand to embrace this dynamic power to live! I much prefer: '**G**od's **R**ighteousness, **A**nd **C**ontinuous **E**mpowering'.

Our labour. The Scriptures are equally clear that we have a vital part to play. We're not told to 'let go'; on the contrary 'the Kingdom advances as forceful men lay hold of it' (Matt 11:12). We are called to take hold of that for which Christ Jesus took hold of us (Phil 3:12) and to take hold of the life that is truly life (1 Tim 6:19). Throughout the New Testament we see constant exhortations to hold fast, and to press on. Paul talks to the Corinthians about the importance of 'strict training' (1 Cor 9:25). We have the responsibility to make godly choices and to trust God for the power that enables us to live out those choices. Sometimes making those choices is difficult; we struggle and wrestle because we are in the process of combating the influence of the world, the old nature and the enemy.

The 'let go and let God' school rejects the idea of effort: it is labelled as 'striving' and regarded as synonymous with legalism. But the Scriptures do not equate effort with legalism. Paul sternly warns his readers to reject legalism and clearly exhorts them to 'make every effort'. Paul brilliantly encapsulates the disciple's lifestyle as he writes to the Colossians, 'I labour, struggling with all His energy which so powerfully works within me.' (Col 1:29). Peter too speaks of the 'divine power that gives us everything we need for life' and two verses later urges his readers to 'make every effort' (2 Pet 1:3,5). To illustrate: I can try to saw through a thick piece of mahogany with a blunt hand-saw and I will quickly tire. I can have a powered circular saw and wait for it to cut the wood by itself . . . and be disappointed. Or I can plug it into the mains, switch it on and cut the wood with it. In the end God's plan for his children, from Adam onwards, has been to work together with Him, learning the family business. He has never wanted His children to remain babies forever. He doesn't want us to be passengers, uninvolved, not contributing. He wants us to learn to accept responsibility, discovering a sense of ownership, trusting in His resources, becoming more intimate with Him by working as a team. These are all part of the dynamics of growing up as children of God, being disciples, changing into His likeness. We cannot become like God by embracing passivity, since He never does.

The corporate dimension

If we are to understand how disciples grow and change we need to recognise that God's chosen framework is a corporate one. Western culture has, for centuries, focused on individualism and sadly this has infiltrated our theology. Often we think of salvation in personal terms. Of course, each person is unique, and every individual needs to make a personal response to Jesus to be born again. But we are born again into a family; we are born into a church, a gathering, a body, a building with many stones. The Scriptures use numerous images to emphasise that discipleship is not about 'me', it's about 'us'.

It is common to hear the idea that 'You don't have to go to church to be a Christian'. But this is simply unbiblical: to be a follower of Christ is inescapably to be part of a church, to belong to a community of God's people. The 'Lone Ranger' Christian may get to heaven but he will face great difficulty in apprehending the fullness of life that God has made available to him. It's in the corporate body that we learn to love, where we struggle and wrestle to value those who are different from ourselves. It's in the corporate body that we see our own weak-nesses clearly. It's also in the corporate body that we learn from others, learn to deploy our gifts and to serve. It's in the corpo-rate body that we learn to face issues instead of running away, and where our characters are developed. As Paul explains, some dimensions of our Christian identity can only be defined in the context of a body, joined to the other parts to complete the whole (1 Cor 12; Eph 4:16). This is a serious challenge to us all: even where Christians are meeting together there's a world of difference between a 'gathering' and a body in the biblical sense.

A new attitude to trouble

We live in a society that places a very high premium on comforts – physical, mental, emotional and financial. In this value system problems and troubles are seen essentially in a negative light. They are to be avoided, fended off or disposed of as quickly as possible; they are seen as a violation of the right to happiness. Even for Christians it's easy to absorb this attitude.

But the Kingdom of God works on radically different principles. God's primary goal for His disciples is not happiness directly but transformation into His likeness. As we become like Christ we become truly fulfilled and happy as human beings. The Scriptures teach us that God frequently uses troubles, hardship, persecution and even suffering as a tool for transforming us into His likeness. God has the awesome capacity to work all things together for good for those who love Him (Rom 8:28). When we face trouble we have a choice – we can ask ourselves questions such as 'Why me?' and 'How can I escape this most rapidly?' If we go down this route we probably remain unchanged. Alternatively, we can ask, 'How is the Lord going to use this to change me? How can I learn from what is happening?' When we use this approach we open wide the door for God to strengthen and mature us.

Change is practical

Finally, I think we need to take hold of the idea that change within us is basically a very practical business. One of the key weaknesses of the Western Church is the tendency to divorce 'spirituality' from 'normal life'; and in the UK the predominance of middle-class culture in our churches has encouraged us to talk about our spirituality in abstract, conceptual terms rather than concrete specifics. The New Testament is a practical manual written in market-place Greek for ordinary people of many cultures to change their lives to be more like Jesus. We so often spiritualise and abstract what are essentially practical instructions and tools for doing a job. When Paul tells his readers to 'Take every thought captive', he is not talking in vague philosophical terms – he is telling them to find practical means to stop thinking in unhealthy ways and start thinking in healthy patterns. Whenever we see plain instructions in the New Testament we should look for plain ways of implementing them. Very often this will involves developing godly habits, changing old patterns of thought, speech, behaviour and relationships. Building godly habits usually involves unfashionable ideas such as repetition, and the hard work of exercising our self-control. 'Sow a habit, reap a change', the adage goes, and often sowing a habit begins simply with repeating a straightforward step. This is such an important point that to illustrate it I've included a case study, a personal testimony of how the Lord changed me and set me free from stress, pressure and anxiety.

Case study: The Stressed Pastor

The subject

The Lord's agenda was to tackle my problems with stress and anxiety.

The goal

The Lord reminded me of His promises to His children, that life to the full means living without worry (Matt 6); knowing His peace and not having a troubled heart (John 14:27); being confident, reigning in life (Rom 5:17); rejoicing always (Phil 4:4).

My situation

Leading a small, inner city, multi-racial congregation, with a number of special needs members, had taken its toll. Although I enjoyed my work I often felt under pressure, as though there was never enough time. At times I felt on the edge of what I could cope with, often facing demands that seemed to exceed my available resources. My devotional life was always under pressure. All of this made me feel tired, prone to irritability, low in confidence, and with a tendency to negative thinking. There were fluctuations of course; sometimes I felt fine, at other times as though I was sinking fast, although I always worked hard at presenting a positive face to the world, rather like the orchestra on the Titanic.

What God said and did

First of all, the Lord made a promise, from a Scripture:

> Forget the former things; do not dwell on the past. See, I am doing a new thing! Now it springs up; do you not perceive it? I am making a way in the desert and streams in the wasteland (Isaiah 43:18–19).

To the question 'Do you not perceive it?' my answer was initially 'No!', but two weeks later I became aware that God was doing something, making power available for me to change. Over about a week, He gave me practical tools and disciplines to apply His power to these areas of my life that would release me and help me to stay free. As you'll see, they're not complex, and indeed they were familiar ideas to me, but now I had a better understanding of my partnership with Him, His resources, and my own responsibility to work hard to apply that power.

What I did

• *Focusing in*. The Lord taught me to live one moment at a time, to concentrate purely on what I was doing there and then. Prior to this, whatever I was doing, I was thinking and worrying about all the other things I *had* to do later, or *ought* to be doing now! God reminded me that He provided manna sufficient only for one day at a time. The Lord's prayer carries the same idea:

daily bread. Jesus teaches that each day has enough worries of its own. Applying this principle to early 21st Century urban life, the Holy Spirit empowers us for what we're doing *now*. We don't have an allotment of grace to spread throughout the day, rather we look to God for strength for each new task. Instead of mentally juggling all the tasks ahead of me, I disciplined myself to give my full and exclusive attention to what I was doing. When I walked the kids to school, that's all I did; when I was shopping or answering a phone call, or preparing a sermon, that's all I thought about.

• *Planning*. The Lord told me to be disciplined about planning. Planning takes time, and previously I had often succumbed to the temptation to drop it to make time for the things I knew needed doing. The Lord reminded me that time is a valuable resource and that I needed to be sure that I was doing the Father's will; in fact, there's not much point in doing anything else. I was to set time aside with Him every day specifically to plan. Also, consistent with the point above, I was to plan only in my planning time, never at any other time.

• *Taking thoughts captive.* God reminded me of the Scripture that calls us to 'Take every thought captive' (2 Cor 10:5). I had to learn to think about what I was thinking about! I guess that most people have 'foreground' thinking, which is whatever we're mainly focused on, but behind that there's a constant murmur of 'background' thinking. Quite a lot of my background thoughts were anxious, fear-based, negative, or contrary to what God had been saying, such as obsessively planning ahead for the day. Basically I practised spotting any thoughts, background or foreground, that were inconsistent with life to the full, and overwrote them with something healthier. With practice I've become more adept at recognising them and dealing with them ruthlessly. It has become something of a sport.

• *Fixing your mind.* Hebrews 3:1 tells us to fix our thoughts on Jesus, and this is the counterpart to taking thoughts captive. I worked on this in two ways. Firstly, I consciously opened myself to Jesus as I performed my daily tasks, disciplining myself to dwell on 'that which is noble, pure, lovely and excellent' (Phil 4:8). This was much easier having eliminated all the worrying and planning ahead that used to occupy that mental space. Secondly, I used post-it notes around the house to remind me of principles and truths that God was teaching me: some of these were Scriptures, others were phrases from films or adverts or whatever God had used to teach me a particular point. Constant exposure through repetition was very helpful. I noticed that a lot of my unhelpful thoughts were patterns that were so well established as to seem normal; but constant exposure to truth helped me to expose them, much as bank clerks through their constant handling of genuine notes quickly identify the one which is false.

• *Humour.* God told me to keep a sharp eye on my sense of humour, because often I was using humour to deal with situations that made me feel negative or worried. Sometimes my jokes and humorous remarks were an early warning system to tell me that there were some things I should talk to God about.

• *Physical disciplines.* The Lord said that I wasn't fit enough, physically. I began to do light training about three times a week. What I found was that not only did I feel healthier, more energetic and better equipped for life, but being disciplined physically was a very positive way of reinforcing disciplines in the other parts of my life I've referred to above. I know from previous experience that I don't have sufficient motivation to take regular exercise because I 'ought to'. But doing it for the Lord, to be better equipped to serve Him, and seeing the knock-on benefits in other areas of my life has given me a vision that has enabled me to sustain it. God also said that I should walk more slowly, and change my posture. I was prone to hurrying everywhere, head down, shoulders slightly hunched. This was reinforcing a sense of being anxious, on the defensive. Changing this physical pattern has proved a helpful part of the process of the renewing of my mind.

• *Lifestyle disciplines.* Similarly, the Lord told me to be more disciplined about what I eat, and about getting to bed on time. I had developed the bad parental habit of eating the kids' left-over food as well as my own, so as not to waste it. God said that eating it when I didn't need it or enjoy it was just as wasteful. Evenings are my favourite time of day, and I had fallen into bad habits of very late nights. Changing these habits has reduced anxiety and released more energy.

• *Celebration.* The Lord pointed out that I had become too serious, too absorbed in mental work. He told me to take time off purely to relax, to do things I enjoyed doing. I was to practise celebration so that I might be more like Him, and represent Him more fully to people who don't know Him. I started to take visits to the theatre, and art galleries. I also found that as the level of obsessive worrying decreased, I was able to enjoy God and worship Him in everything I was doing.

• *Responsibility.* I was very prone to worry about things over which I had no control and which were not my responsibilities. The Lord reminded me that He would build His church (Matt 16:18); that while one plants and another waters, it's God who brings growth (1 Cor 3:7) and that He is in control. He also taught me that I should allow others to carry the responsibility appropriate to them. For me to carry it was not only wrongly stressful for me, but even more seriously, was denying them an opportunity for growth.

Feedback/outcome

• *For myself.* Since the Lord began this work, I've been progressively set free from pressure and stress. I feel happier and more relaxed. I feel more fully myself; much healthier. I seem to have more time available, and I seem to get a great deal more accomplished in the course of a day. I have more confidence, and feel much more that I am reigning in life. An unexpected bonus is that God seems to have broken my fear of crowds. There is work involved in following the instructions God gave me; I struggle with His energy, although as it becomes more habitual it becomes easier. When I neglect His instructions my stress levels soon begin to rise. The Bible is right: life to the full is worth working for!

Sometimes people have asked me 'How do you know if you're relying on God's strength or your own, especially when doing it right can be a struggle?' I suspect that in the longer term discernment grows. For now, I've simply chosen to assume that if I'm doing the right things for the right motives, God will empower. The key is to keep checking motives. If I'm doing the right things but with legalistic motives, trying to earn God's favour, or repay His kindness, then I'm likely to find myself running on batteries. If my aim is to be more like Him, to live life more fully by living it more for His glory, then I assume I'm connected to the mains. After all, He's a faithful and loving Father who keeps His promises.

• *For my family.* My wife says that I've become much better company. We have quality time together because I'm less distracted. She has also felt freer to pursue new avenues in her own life. Previously she was reluctant to do anything that might increase the pressure on me, but now because I have available energy, she's able to ask for support without feeling guilty, or risking an irritable response. My relationship with my children has improved because of a new sense of fun, and because I give them full attention when we're together.

• *The Church.* Church members have commented that I'm more relaxed. This has, they say, improved my preaching. They also feel they are 'getting through to me' when we're talking. Spending more time in God's presence has helped me when ministering and praying for people.

• *Other relationships.* My not-yet-Christian friends know me less intimately than family or church members, so I expect the changes are less immediately noticeable. Nevertheless, some have commented that I always seem positive and on top of things, and wanted to know why. I seem to have had more evangelistic conversations since these changes began.

SUMMARY

The process of becoming more like Jesus, more contagious, is about change. Inner transformation will not be affected by legalism or by an attitude of 'let go and let God', but by a partnership with the Holy Spirit, in which we are willing to labour, using His energy which so powerfully works within us.

God's framework for change is counter-cultural; it is corporate not individualistic; it sees problems as a vehicle for His purposes rather than something negative; and it focuses not on vague generalities but on practical, specific application in our lives.

Chapter 4

TOOLS FOR TRANSFORMATION

Out of the chrysalis

I have a CD ROM encyclopaedia, and sometimes my children sit on my knee and we browse, seeing what we can discover. They particularly like the video clips. One of their favourites is watching a butterfly emerging from its chrysalis. I've seen it many times now, but I'm still fascinated because of its power as a metaphor for disciple-making. Paul tells the Christians in Ephesus (Eph 4:22–24) to put off the old self and to put on the new self. The butterfly, of course, was formerly a caterpillar; it underwent a form of death, and came to life as a new creature. As Christians we have been born again, a transformation has taken place! There is no going back; we have been born of an imperishable seed, literally sperm, of God (1 Pet 1:23). The old nature has been killed, crucified on the cross, its authority and power broken. But the butterfly, although transformed, must wrestle and struggle out of the cocoon, a dead shell that constrains it, in order to be free. And it needs to spread its wings and learn how to fly. As disciples we too may find that we still have a shell of our own life wrapped around us, its power broken on the Cross, but nevertheless constraining us. We also need to wrestle to break free from it so as we can realise our potential. Like the butterfly, we need to explore these wonderful new capabilities; to learn how to fly.

The limitations of counselling

How do we break out of those parts of the chrysalis shell that constrict us? What are the mechanics for bringing about change within ourselves? One route that has been explored extensively in recent years is counselling. In the secular world there has been an explosion of interest in counselling, therapy and support groups, as people recognise the pain and problems of their lives and look for solutions. Typically, where society leads, the church tends to plod along afterwards, often with a frightening lack of discernment. Across the UK church we have seen a significant take-up of counselling and therapy in one form or another. Many churches have set up counselling teams, and regularly refer members to outside therapy groups. But the impact is more than simply *activity*: we need to recognise that there is a whole set of related *values* that are exerting influence in our society, values that are promulgated through TV chat shows, magazines and the like. Therapy culture, if I can so term it, is inevitably shaping the worldview of many Christians, whether or not they have received counselling themselves.

This has gone largely unchallenged in our churches. It's true that questions have been raised relating to issues such as which model to use and how to improve quality control. The result has been to push Christian counsellors towards more rigorous training, and to acquire secular qualifications. This is well and good, but is essentially tinkering with the superstructure. We need to look deeper, and be prepared to ask the big questions that challenge the whole foundation. To what extent is the counselling and therapy model actually biblical? How effective is it at making disciples who live life to the full? These questions are difficult to answer because counselling practice within and outside churches varies so widely, and because therapy culture is so complex. A full examination is obviously beyond the scope of this book. Nevertheless I think it's important to highlight some of the concerns that have arisen from practical experience across a number of churches.

• *The blame culture.* The emphasis in therapy culture of finding and analysing root causes has prompted many people to abdicate personal responsibility. It's both tempting and convenient to be able to put the blame on parents, traumatic experiences or demons, but it doesn't bring either freedom or maturity. Good counselling emphasises the acceptance of responsibility, but many people seem to have picked up only half the message.

• *The identity issue.* Therapy culture has spawned an ever-increasing number of recognised disorders and syndromes. Some are still the subject of much debate, but the point is that giving a set of responses a label in this way can tempt people to legitimise unacceptable behaviour on the basis that they can't help themselves because of their condition. There is a danger too of starting to define one's identity in terms of a particular dysfunction: 'My name is Jane, I am co-dependant'. I don't deny the importance of facing the reality about ourselves with honesty, but it is critical that we understand the distinction between our old nature and our new nature. It may be true that our old nature is co-dependant, but in God we find our true identity: a royal priesthood, more than conquerors, children of the King! Whereas therapy culture can encourage a victim mentality, the Bible's message is that in Christ we reign in life (Rom 5:17).

• *Problem orientation.* Counselling and therapy are basically problem-centred. They begin because someone perceives a problem in their lives and seeks help. This can become dangerously one-sided; preoccupation with one's problems can quickly degenerate into introspection and self-centredness. It can promote the perspective that the goal of life is to have one's needs met, and God becomes therapy with a spiritual dimension, the divine problem solver. I don't deny for one moment that God is a loving Father who meets our needs; but the crucial point is that our view of life must be God-centred, not man-centred (or man/problem-centred,) in order to be healthy. This highlights the point made in chapter 2: the need for a radical re-direction of our theology that puts God and ourselves in the proper place. Ultimately God isn't there to meet our needs; we are here to glorify Him.

Another difficulty with problem orientation is simply the imbalance. Personal transformation into the likeness of Christ is as much about putting on the new nature as it is about putting off the old. We run the risk of trying to heal our old nature when we should in fact be dying to it.

• *Dependence.* The mechanics and structures of counselling raise problems in themselves. There is a well-known risk of the client becoming dependent on the counsellor; the relationship is an intimate one and the roles of help-giver and help-receiver are clear-cut. The risk, of course, is that the client becomes less well equipped to tackle life and becomes 'hooked' either on the counsellor or the therapy process. It is not unusual to hear of people stressed-out because their counsellor has gone on holiday, denying them their weekly 'fix'.

• *Detachment.* There is a flip side to this coin. Recognising the danger of dependence, most counsellors work to principles and guidelines that maintain professional detachment. In recognition of their power in the relationship and the client's vulnerability there is great caution about being directive; there is limited accountability; and the counselling is limited to set times and places. Unfortunately, clear direction, accountability and ongoing support are, in my view, paramount to the process of change. And whereas counselling is restricted to dialogue focussing on the problem, I am convinced that people-changing requires a more integrated, holistic approach that involves giving as well as receiving, action as well as talk, and vision sowing as well as problem solving. Particularly where a Christian is receiving counselling outside the church, experience shows that it's extremely difficult to integrate it with the wider pattern of pastoral care.

• *Professionalism.* It is not only a question of the effect on individuals: therapy culture can also be corrosive to church values. It is quite a short step to see counselling or specialist help as the answer to every problem. The effect of this is to make church members feel redundant, unqualified and incompetent to help. Friendship is devalued because it isn't a professional qualification. Fellowship decays to superficiality with the real stuff of our lives happening behind closed doors. In short, the role of the body to shape the lives of its members is drastically diminished.

In a number of ways then, therapy culture and the counselling model are inconsistent with the biblical theology of discipleship. These are serious problems and limitations. I am not denying that counselling and therapy have some role to play, nor do I want to undervalue those Christians who are thoughtfully, prayerfully, lovingly and skilfully engaged in this work. But we have to make sure that we have appropriate expectations. Is counselling the vehicle for filling our churches with contagious Christians? The evidence so far suggests not. We need the courage to face this honestly and look in new directions. It's a question once again of being willing to change our thinking patterns. The Bible, of course, gives us plenty of material for doing just that, and I want to explore some of the principles that we find there.

Looking at the template

To be effective in helping people to be transformed into the likeness of Christ we need to start from the right place. And the right place must surely be a template of what humanity is intended to be, not 'What seems to be the problem?'.

If we understand what humans are intended to be, we can see more clearly all those areas that need to change, not only those which present themselves as problems. We all know that patterns of thought or behaviour developed over a lifetime can seem entirely 'normal' until, often with a shock, we realise they are defective. If we start from perceived problems, rather than a template, we may well miss these vital areas.

When we're working with a template we have a more balanced and biblical approach to transformation; we don't stop simply when the pain or problem has been addressed, we continue until we have laid hold of the fullness of life in that area. We put on the new nature, as well as put off the old. Working with a template provides a better reference point to see the progress we're making and whether the efforts we are making are proving fruitful.

The key is to change our goal. Instead of seeing the *relief of discomfort* as our target, we need to reorientate completely, so that our aim is to *become more like Christ*. This is absolutely critical, because sometimes the process of becoming more like Jesus may actually increase our pain and discomfort. The writer to the Hebrews comments that they hadn't yet resisted sin to the point of shedding blood (12:4). This indicates what a gritty battle we must sometimes fight to shed the old nature, resist the enemy, and grow in maturity and holiness. It is only when we start from this point that we can change our attitude to crisis and disaster. A problem-based approach is looking for a way out of the situation, a way to restore comfort as soon as possible. But if our goal is Christlikeness then our response to crisis is to ask how God will use it to help us grow and mature.

Putting on the new nature, putting off the old

When we have a biblical model of what humanity is intended to be we are also in a better position to see just what has gone wrong, to see the effects of the Fall on human beings. If we can gain understanding of the basic underlying patterns of the way people are malfunctioning, then it becomes much easier to make sense of the tangled mess we find within ourselves!

Our re-balanced theology has a significant impact on the business of living by our new nature and putting off the old. We understand that once born again we've begun an exciting journey into freedom. We realise that putting on the new nature enables us to fulfil our destiny to be children of God, in the likeness of Christ, ruling with Him. We grasp that living for God instead of for self is the way to fulfilment, healthiness, wholeness and joy. Two important changes follow. Firstly, we begin to see our old nature more clearly. Our old nature disguises itself as 'normality', but we see that selfishness, legalism, and attitudes that suppress and constrict life, while pervasive, are actually abnormal and subnormal. The second change is in our motivation. The more we grasp what we're intended to be, the more we realise that the old nature acts as chains around our feet, stopping us from running. We develop a righteous indignation, a godly resolve not to tolerate it! This is precisely the image that the writer to the Hebrews uses: '. . . let us throw off everything that hinders and the sin that so easily entangles, and let us run with perseverance the race marked out for us' (Heb 12:1).

I'd like to illustrate these points with testimonies from two people in my church. These testimonies have emerged as we've worked on these areas of our understanding:

Tom

'I wanted to be more disciplined in my prayers, but I realised that it was hard to be disciplined in this area of my life when I was ill-disciplined in another area, my eating habits. Something has really changed here. I used to say to myself: "I mustn't eat that junk food, I mustn't, I mustn't . . . Oh dear". But since I've been thinking about life to the full, my attitude has changed completely. Now when temptation comes I say: "I'm not going to be played for a fool by a cream bun! I want to live in true freedom to make choices, not be pushed around by temptation." The great thing is that now I've broken the power of its temptation (after practising), I feel free to eat a cream bun or whatever from time to time and do so with an attitude of thanksgiving and celebration instead of the misery of guilt and defeat. And learning to be disciplined in this area has rubbed off on my prayer life, which has become much more dynamic.'

Lynn

'I've started to see my old nature more clearly. When I see how awful it is, and how it wants to trap me and destroy my freedom in Christ, I get angry. When I start to feel self-condemnation, I think to myself "Oh yes, this is a favourite line my old nature uses", and instead of going under, I push right back! Actually I have a motto for these situations: "Kill, kill, kill!". I've also learned that my old nature is what Satan tries to play on, but I discovered an idea to tackle this from watching *Star Trek*. There's an episode where Captain Picard's ship is under heavy fire from an enemy cruiser. Just when all seems lost, he has the inspiration to make a light-speed hop, timed to coincide with the enemy's fire. The enemy cruiser fires on the ghost image of Picard's ship. Picard in reality is behind the enemy cruiser, takes it by surprise and destroys it. That's what I try to do: Satan targets me, so I make sure I'm not there. I leave my old nature behind, and the real me, living in my new nature is somewhere else, firing all my phasers at Satan and my old nature. I guess I'm learning something about what the Bible means when it talks about dying to self, putting off the old nature, and spiritual warfare.'

Ephesians 4:24 instructs us to put off the old nature which is being corrupted by its evil desires, and put on the new nature which is created to be like God in true righteousness and holiness. Colossians 3:5,10 conveys the same message: we are to put to death what belongs to our earthly nature, and 'put on the new self, which is being renewed in knowledge in the image of its Creator'. Healthy motivation for changing our lifestyle comes when we see clearly the stark choice facing us: corruption or Christlikeness. As the testimonies above demonstrate, when we are born again we are for the first time truly free to choose; through His empowering we can choose life. If we don't, we choose death. Not too hard to decide.

God's agenda

Putting our theology into practice also affects the way we set our agenda for change. If our aim is to solve our problems, meet our needs and remove discomfort, we set our own agenda, usually starting with what hurts most. But when we fix our aim on becoming like Jesus and living in fullness of life, it follows that we need to allow God to set the agenda. When we're working in partnership with Him, it makes sense that the starting point is to listen. God's priorities for changing us may not accord with our own! If we work to our own agenda we find ourselves running on batteries. When we're in line with God, then we work with mains power. It's important to remember that God's desire to change us, to liberate us and grow us, is far greater than our own. He will tell us where to change, how to change and provide us with the power to change.

The 'wholing' community

The 'healing community' would be a more familiar term, but for me it carries connotations of curing sickness – a problem-solving slant that, as you'll have gathered by now, I'm keen we should escape. People sometimes talk of church as a hospital for those in need, but we have to see it as so much more: a place for training, nurturing, developing new capabilities, discovering our true potential.

The individualism of our culture has been instrumental in steering us down the counselling route, but biblically disciple-making is a corporate, community process. The New Testament is saturated with 'one-anothers': encourage one another, edify one another, seek after what is good for one another, stimulate one another to love and good deeds, admonish one another, serve one another. Paul repeatedly refers to the church as a body; it is as part of a whole that each member is built up.

When we're being changed within the community of God's people we're less prone to unhealthy dependence because we're being helped by a number of people, not one counsellor. We find it easier to give as well as receive, because we're helping other people to grow. We can receive the support and help we need because we are not limited to a half-hour session. We can draw on a much wider range of help because God may change us through people with prophetic ministry, or those with words of wisdom, or mercy, in other words a diversity of gifts that far exceeds those of any one person.

In the church community we can take the risk of bringing clear direction, specific, practical advice and accountability. Counsellors have to be wary of this because of the risk in a one-to-one relationship of creating an unhealthy level of control. But within the church community the risk is diffused because each member is part of a web of relationships, all of which are sharing in the task of bringing change.

Putting it into practice: life-changing in small groups

So far in this chapter I've covered general principles. I now want to turn to practical application.

In my own church we've found our cell groups a very effective forum for some aspects of the personal transformation that is central to disciple-making. We follow the classical cell model, using the four W's: Welcome, Worship, Word and Witness[1]. Outlined below is the approach we use for our 'Word' element. We use a model that has six parts. This may sound complicated but in practice the steps are fairly straightforward.

1. Choosing the subject

We find the 'Word' section in our small group meetings particularly effective in two areas of transformation. One of these is developing 'heart' knowledge, closing the gap between what we know in our minds and what we actually believe: an example would be 'knowing the fatherhood of God'. The other is learning to live God's way in our everyday lives. This is important for three reasons. First, it causes us to engage not only with abstract ideas, but also with the concrete and practical, helping to break down the spiritual/secular divide in our thinking. Secondly, in a progressively post-Christian society, many people are simply ignorant of the basic principles of healthy living. We need to know what we know and not assume that others know it! Subjects that we tackle in this category include food, managing money, leisure, how to make friends, honesty, and handling anger. Thirdly, addressing issues of everyday life can help to bridge the gap to non-book culture groups.

2. The template

Using a 'discovery' approach rather than straight teaching works best for us. Basically we set homework: we ask everyone in the group to think about the subject in question and work out what we're aiming for, what life to the full looks like in this area. In other words, we're drawing up a template. This means reading the Bible, thinking, praying, and using the imagination. Doing it this way builds a sense of accountability and taking responsibility. It also starts to create a sense of vision, an idea of where we're going that everyone feels they own. When the group meets the following week, we ask for feedback and draw up a picture of what God has destined for His people. We try to express this not only in terms of abstract principles but images, phrases and examples too. Somehow this generates a rounded, three-dimensional picture that engages everyone. It is often at this stage that people rediscover what they had taken for granted, or have their vision extended by what others have said. Obviously, during this feedback group leaders are testing everything against the Scriptures. The picture that emerges from this is usually very exciting and motivating! As an illustration, this is the template from one of our groups on the theme of 'Knowing the fatherhood of God.'

When we truly know the fatherhood of God, it will be a relationship in which:

- we know that He sees us as valuable more than useful
- we feel encouraged, provided for, loved (Phil 4:19)
- we hero-worship, we want to grow up to be like Him
- we feel totally secure (Rom 8:38–39)
- we feel intimate with Him (Eph 3:12)
- we know we are loved unconditionally
- we recognise and happily accept our complete dependence on Him
- we know that He is there, close by, all the time (Acts 17:27)
- we know that we please Him, that He likes us and accepts us
- we know that He's not disappointed in us, or disapproving of us (Eph 1:5)
- we know He's in control: Dad can handle it!
- we know His never-ending kindness towards us, His comfort
- we receive His discipline and correction positively, seeing His loving purpose (Heb 12:5–11)
- we have a sense of excitement, joyful anticipation: 'Dad's coming home!' (Rom 8:15)
- we know that we have a purpose
- we experience His equipping, helping and empowering (Matt 7:11)

- we know He will give us the space to grow and develop
- we feel relaxed, spontaneous, creative, and enjoy His company
- we know that we can talk to Him about absolutely everything
- we know that He bends down to listen to us (Hosea 11:4)
- we experience His generosity which goes beyond meeting our needs
- we have time for Him, and know that He has time for us
- we are at peace
- we are completely secure, as He is faithful and trustworthy (Ps 89:1)

3. Testimony

It's exciting to have a vision of God's destination for us in specific areas of our life. But it's also very helpful to nurture faith by seeing changes that God has already brought about. So, giving testimony is our next stage. Everyone is encouraged to say what they have already learned or how they have changed in this particular area. It's helpful to see that God is already on the move and it's always encouraging to hear how God has changed someone in an area where we ourselves are struggling. We have found it surprising and exciting to hear the extraordinarily diverse ways in which God has worked. Here are some examples, again on the theme of the fatherhood of God:

- God taught Ali about His fatherly generosity by some extraordinary examples of His provision;
- Lee was deeply moved by a sculpture she bought, and it showed her how pleased God is with her;
- Simone found that keeping a prayer journal helped her to realise that He's never far away even when she couldn't feel His presence;
- God taught Winston to have confidence in Him through an advertising logo;
- Janet grew in her security in Him as she prayed;

- Stuart caught the vision of working in partnership with God for His purposes by rubbing shoulders with other Christians at conferences;
- God taught Lily about freedom from fear and anxiety by helping her to take practical steps of faith;
- Les learned that it's OK to change one step at a time, as God took him through a series of difficult experiences;
- God taught Gill that He knows her by name through the amazing provision of her favourite bar of chocolate in a remote village in the Far East;
- God taught Smita about His love for her through an experience of serious illness;
- Zeb grew in assurance that she could rely completely on God's strength by reading Scriptures on that subject;
- God spoke to Penny through a series of dreams to tell her that He doesn't compare her unfavourably with others;
- God taught Olu about the Father's authority through an episode of Miami Vice;
- Jordan felt his knowledge that he is acceptable to God had grown gradually over several years.

(All names changed)

Testimonies of this nature can be very effective in helping us to discard our blinkers, to shatter presuppositions. We have such a tendency to put God in a box and we need to challenge it constantly.

The whole purpose is to help everyone grasp that reaching the goal is not unattainable; in fact quite the reverse: it's inevitable and God has already begun.

4. The Agenda

The next stage is for everyone to line up their own lives against the template to see where the gaps are. Most people already have a pretty good idea of this as a by-product of producing the template together. But there is a crucial extra step: we ask everyone to pray and ask God what He wants to work on in their lives. The idea is to give everyone habitual experience of allowing God to set the agenda, rather than allowing our own needs or problems to dictate. We may minister to someone in an area where they are already strong if that is God's leading. This is the whole issue: we do *whatever is for His glory*, not what makes us comfortable. We gain practical experience in listening to Him. People can sometimes feel intimidated by this practical exercise of listening to God: 'What if I don't hear Him?' Our basic position is that if we earnestly listen but don't hear anything, we should assume that the Lord is giving the choice back to us until He says otherwise. Everyone in the group feeds back and the group leaders make a list; this becomes the basis for ministry in future weeks.

5. Ministry

Each week we choose a couple of people to whom the group will minister. Before ministry begins, we run through the goals or vision again as a reminder. Simple repetition is immensely powerful in rooting ideas in people's minds. We ask those to be prayed for if they wish to update the areas they identified as on God's agenda for them. Then we wait on God in silence for about five minutes, or longer if we can manage it, after which we begin ministering. We encourage everyone to participate and to bring prayers, scriptures, prophetic pictures, and words of advice. We encourage the use of every day language and practical illustrations. Recently in one of our ministry sessions someone felt that the Lord wanted the person being prayed for to watch a particular film to help her grasp a point about God being in control.

6. Follow-up

The final stage is critical; we invite those who have been prayed for in previous weeks to give testimony as to what has happened. Again this is an issue of accountability, but not only for the individual – for the group as well. The point is that if there hasn't been change, then we are committed as a group to minister again and continue supporting that person. It reinforces the idea that the focus is on real change, not merely on going through a programme. Often the testimonies are very encouraging to the group.

Where change has taken place one of our key questions is 'Do you think that the change in you is noticeable to those around you?' It's vital to remind the group that one of our overriding priorities is to be so transformed that we are contagious as Christians, provoking those around us who don't know God by the quality and fullness of life we have. Sometimes the very act of feeding back to the group gives a ready-made testimony that has a habit of finding its way into conversations with not-yet-Christian friends. This is perhaps one of the few benefits of living in a 'therapy culture': people are both more interested in and more open to discuss personal growth, especially when they can see the evidence themselves. When our testimony is current rather than historic, it has a freshness that is highly attractive, and an immediacy that conveys relevance.

Depending on the size of the group and the nature of the subject, we might stay with the same topic for a number of weeks. This is a marked contrast to our previous small group practice of looking at a different subject almost every week. Having tried both, I personally have no doubts that going more slowly but seeing real change is a far better route to disciple-making. We also ring the changes: after a few weeks on a theme such as knowing the father heart of God, we switch to a specific lifestyle area such as managing money. The same model can also be based on a chapter or two of Scripture; it gives a template that covers a wider range of different aspects of life to the full and slightly more diversity in the ministry and feedback, but the principles are just the same.

SUMMARY

Christians have undergone metamorphosis. The power of the old self has been put to death on the Cross. We are called in Scripture to shed this old self and to put on our new self. In other words, we are called to be transformed into the likeness of Christ, to come into maturity and to realise the fullness of life He has given us. How does this take place? There has been extensive use of counselling in recent years, but as a model it has a number of flaws and limitations, particularly in its problem-orientated approach. A better starting point is knowing what God intends us to be, understanding the shortfall, and seeing that the process of becoming whole takes place in a corporate context, the body of Christ. Small groups can be effective tools in this process.

Chapter 5

SPIRITUAL FITNESS

Using the disciplines

Run. Wrestle. Labour. Struggle. Press on. These are just a handful of the exhortations in the New Testament. And they tell us one thing: that spiritual fitness isn't an optional extra; it is vital to the fulfilment of our calling. It's a responsibility we bear for ourselves. How can we break out of the pattern of two steps forward and then one back? How can we lay hold of change and build it into our lives? How do we develop the spiritual suppleness, endurance and readiness that we long for?

Throughout the centuries, many Christians, especially in the Catholic, Orthodox and Celtic traditions have seen spiritual disciplines such as fasting, silence, solitude, meditation, contemplation, simplicity and secrecy as a vital part of the answer to these questions.

In general, the Protestant Church has given less weight to the practice of these disciplines, and most Charismatic Evangelicals give them low priority. Having said that, there are signs of change: in recent years titles such as Richard Foster's *Celebration of Discipline* and Gordon MacDonald's *Ordering Your Private World*[1] have sold widely. But still there is a lot of ground to recover. Why does this gap exist? Why is there still an attitude of caution and suspicion?

67

Abuses and extremes. It is true that historically some have taken spiritual disciplines to extremes, such as the early Christian ascetics who expressed their dedication by living on the tops of pillars with the most meagre supply of food and the barest necessities of clothing. In the 4th Century Simeon Stylites lived atop his sixty-foot pillar for thirty years. It is hard to escape the conclusion that there was a measure of competition in such asceticism that speaks more of pride than humility. It is also difficult to see how either the corporate dimension of Christianity or the outward call of the Great Commission was fulfilled by such a lifestyle. This is not a purely historical phenomenon; in our own times some Christians at the 'super-spiritual' end of the spectrum have adopted fasting, in particular, as an emblem of their zeal and commitment. When the disciplines become spiritual goals in their own right we quickly go off track.

Poor theology. In medieval times spiritual disciplines were sometimes practised in the hope of earning salvation or as a penance, both of which are theological ideas that many of us would vigorously challenge.

Disconnection from real life. A further stumbling block is the perception of the disciplines as irrelevant or unworkable for Christians in everyday life. A common view would be to see them as appropriate to the monastery or perhaps a week's holiday-cum-retreat, but too introspective to play a central role in our walk with Christ.

Discomfort. An obviously unattractive feature of spiritual disciplines is that they often involve discomforts – physical, mental or emotional. This is clearly contrary to the values of our culture, which we as Christians sometimes struggle to escape.

The body. Finally, disciplines such as fasting, silence and solitude involve the body in a significant way. But in the Western

Church, we're reluctant to think of the body in spiritual terms and we're conditioned to think about our physical nature as distinct, separate and peripheral to our spirituality. This reflects the influence on our culture of ancient Greek thinking. We have probably all heard sermons that neatly partition human beings into body, soul and spirit, conveniently echoing the Trinity.

But the scriptural view of the body is radically different from our own Greek-influenced perspective. The Scriptures see human beings holistically: our bodies are intrinsic to our form as human beings and they are a vital element in our spirituality. Paul talks about the war raging in his members (Rom 7:23). Our bodies are members of Christ (1 Cor 6:15); the Holy Spirit brings life to our mortal bodies (Rom 8:11); we are to train our bodies (1 Cor 9:24–27) and we are to offer our bodies as living sacrifices (Rom 12:1). It is significant that in our final form, in the new heaven and new earth, we are not disembodied spirits; rather our bodies are raised imperishable (1 Cor 15: 42).

Using a thoroughly biblical approach to the body we need to challenge negative perspectives on the spiritual disciplines, acknowledging the dangers but not throwing out the baby with the bath water.

The purpose of spiritual disciplines

If we aim to become more like Jesus, it's not going to be enough simply to adopt a set of beliefs; we need to live as He did, seeing His lifestyle as a model for our own. Jesus himself fasted, frequently withdrew to places of silence and solitude and exercised secrecy. I recently skimmed through the Gospels and found forty references to Jesus' use of these disciplines. In giving instructions on fasting Jesus seems to have assumed that it would be part of the disciples' lifestyle (Matt 6: 16–18, Luke 5:35). The Apostle Paul fasted and spent time in isolation in the desert, and there are other references to fasting throughout the

New Testament. The early Fathers likewise, saw spiritual disciplines as the norm for Christian living.

So what are the disciplines for? Clearly they are not forms of penance or one-upmanship. No, a far healthier approach is to see spiritual disciplines as the *means*, not as ends in themselves. They are to Christians what training and practice is to people who enjoy sport; they are not the game itself, but an indispensable preparation. People work hard at training so that they have the freedom to enjoy and excel at their chosen sport. Most footballers, for example, can do fifty press-ups at the drop of a hat. But they don't do press-ups for their own sake; they are not an end in themselves, they are the means, part of the process of building strength and fitness for the true end: playing football to the peak of their ability. Spiritual disciplines work in the same way; their purpose is to equip us for our true goals of loving God and loving people. Paul stresses the importance of training when he compares the Christian lifestyle with that of athletes preparing for the games (1 Cor 9:25, 1 Tim 4:7).

If we keep this perspective we're safeguarded from many of the problems highlighted earlier. If we understand that disciplines are tools, not the job, we will be less likely to take them to unhealthy extremes; less prone to trying to earn God's favour through them, and less likely to fall into the trap of trying to score spiritual status points. In the end, both the manager and the supporters are not impressed by how many press-ups the team can do, but how many games of football they win. Likewise, when we see how powerful the disciplines can be to equip us, we find true motivation to engage in them. Where we wrongly see them as ends in themselves, we find ourselves struggling in a mass of legalistic ought's and should's and quickly grind to a halt.

Fasting

It is clear that fasting is not an end in itself: God provided food for Adam and Eve in abundance; He provided for the Israelites throughout their time in the wilderness; and repeatedly throughout Scripture He affirms His promise to provide food. Psalm 23 reminds us that in the presence of our enemies He lays a table for us. In Revelation, as God's ultimate purposes are unfolded, the children of God are invited to a feast, the Wedding Feast of the Lamb, not a 'spiritual' time of fasting.

But fasting is a valuable tool: it can help us to learn humility before God; and it can remind us of our complete dependence on him. It can help to clear and focus our minds to hear God as we pray. I've found it highly effective in revealing my shallowness when I see how quickly (depressingly!) my behaviour deteriorates as I become hungry. Fasting can help us truly enjoy food when we do eat; to eat with a sense of worship and celebration. Isaiah 68 reminds us that fasting is not the goal in itself: its purpose is to equip us in our true calling to live for truth, justice and righteousness.

Solitude and silence

Likewise, solitude and silence are not goals in themselves: God sets the lonely in families and throughout the Bible we see over and over again the importance of being with other people: family, tribe, nation, church. In Revelation the glimpses of God's destiny for us essentially show multitudes in unity declaring God's praises. Yet solitude and silence are valuable tools in teaching us to seek our identity in Him, not in the opinions of men, and to know our value as a child of God, not as an important figure in the business world, for example. They can help us to learn humility as we discover that we're not as important or indispensable as we sometimes like to think. They can show us how much we hide from God, from others and from ourselves by our constant flow of words, or by living in the noise of ceaseless music and TV.

These principles are vividly captured by William Dalrymple in his book *From the Holy Mountain*,[1] a moving account of the plight of the Middle Eastern Church. He records his discussions with a monk in a desert monastery:

> This evening I had a long conversation with Fr. Dioscuros in the refectory of the guest quarters. As the last light was fading gradually from the sky outside, I asked him about his motives for becoming a monk and why he'd left the comforts of Alexandria for the harsh climate of the desert.
>
> 'Many people think we come to the desert to punish ourselves, 'cause it is hot and dry and difficult to live in,' said Fr. Dioscuros. 'It's not true. We come because we love it here.'
>
> 'What is there to love about the desert?'
>
> 'We love the peace, the silence. When you really want to talk to someone you want to sit together in a quiet place and talk, not be in the midst of a crowd of other people. How can you talk properly in a crowd? So it is with us. We come here because we want to be alone with our God. As St. Anthony once said: "Let your heart be silent, then God will speak".'
>
> 'But you do seem to want to punish yourselves deliberately: the hot, coarse robes you wear, the long Lenten fasts you all undertake . . .'
>
> 'Ah,' said Fr. Dioscuros, 'but you see fasting is not punishment. It is a tool, not an end in itself. It is not easy to communicate with God on a full stomach. When you have had a big meal you cannot concentrate your mind. You want to go to sleep, not to be in church praying. To pray successfully it is better to be a little hungry.'
>
> 'But doing without possessions: isn't that a punishment?'
>
> 'No, it's a choice. For myself I have begun to get rid of many of the things which clutter up my cell. Last week I threw out my chair. I don't need it. Now I sit on the floor. Why should I bother with extra food, with spare clothes, with unnecessary furniture? All you need is a piece of bread and enough covering for the body. The less you have, the less you have to distract you from God. Do you understand?'
>
> I smiled, uncertainly.
>
> 'Well, just look around this room. When I am in here I think that the chair is in the wrong place, I must move it. Or maybe that the

lamp is out of oil, I must fill it. Or . . . or that that shutter is broken and I must get it mended. But in the desert there is just sand. You don't think of anything else; there is nothing to disturb you. It should be the same in a monk's cell. The less there is, the easier it is to talk to God.'

'Do you find it easy?'

'It is never easy, but with practice I find it less difficult,' said Dioscuros. 'The spiritual life is like a ladder. Every day if you are disciplined and make the effort you find you will rise up, understand a little better, find it a little easier to concentrate, find that your mind is wandering less and less. When you pray alone in your cell without distraction you feel as if you are in front of God, as if nothing is coming to you except from God. When you succeed – if you do manage to banish distractions and communicate directly with God – then the compensation outweighs any sufferings or hardships. You feel as if something which was dim is suddenly lighted for you. You feel full of light and pleasure: it is like a blinding charge of electricity.'

'But you don't have to come to the middle of the desert to find an empty room free of distractions. You can find that anywhere: in Cairo, or Alex, or London . . .'

'What you say is true,' said Fr. Dioscuros with a smile. 'You can pray anywhere. After all, God is everywhere, so you can find him everywhere.' He gestured to the darkening sand dunes outside.[2]

(Quoted with permission)

Jesus clearly saw the value of spiritual disciplines as a means of strengthening and equipping. It's no surprise that Jesus' experience in the wilderness comes at the start of his ministry, a time of preparation and training. It is no accident that He chooses to face the temptations of Satan himself when He's in this place of special readiness. Luke 4:14 records that at the end of the forty days Jesus returned to Galilee 'in the power of the Spirit'. Luke also records a time when Jesus' ministry was particularly intense, teaching every day at the temple – a gruelling schedule. Jesus' response wasn't to get plenty of early nights: on the contrary, He spent each night in solitude out on the Mount of Olives (Luke 21:37–38).

The discipline of our thoughts

Spiritual disciplines are exercises that train us. They may involve hard work, perhaps some discomfort of body, mind or emotions, but they bring strength and growth. The Apostle Paul's instructions about our minds are a case in point. He calls for Christians to demolish strongholds, arguments and pretensions, and to take captive every thought to make it obedient to Christ (2 Cor 10:4–5). He tells us to be transformed by the renewing of the mind (Rom 12:2). This is not something we can do casually: it requires work, practice, vigilance and perseverance, but the goal is living by the mind of Christ, our thinking healthy and free.

The challenge we face in achieving this has never been greater. The new millennium sees us in the midst of a communication revolution. Through TV and the Internet, telephones, faxes, radio and satellites we have become a global community. Our generation is experiencing a storm of information, images, ideas, changes and different cultures that is completely unprecedented. More than this, we need to recognise that we're not merely in the data stream, we're actually targeted by it. Every advert that we encounter in newspapers, on TV, on our computers, on the sides of buses, the logos on our clothing, is attempting to manipulate our thinking. Politicians, broadcasters, businessmen, lobbyists, and interest groups are specifically seeking to influence our behaviour: to make us buy, to change our priorities, to persuade us, to win our vote. We're exposed daily to philosophies, cultures, religions and value systems that try to shape us into their mould. The constant bombardment is visual, verbal, conscious, subconscious and subliminal.

In this context Paul's call to spiritual discipline in our thinking was never more relevant than today. Paul instructs the

Roman Church to renew their minds in order not to be squeezed into the world's pattern. (Rom 12:2). Unless we learn to be vigilant in taking thoughts captive and rigorous in testing everything against the benchmark of Scripture, we're in danger of simply being overwhelmed. We need the discipline not to allow ourselves to think certain things: distortions of the truth or attitudes of cynicism, selfishness, and anti-authoritarianism for example. We need to learn the disciplines of self-examination, confession and prayer to cleanse our mind. In the face of this constant barrage, there has never been a time when we've more needed to learn the discipline of fixing our thoughts on Jesus (Heb 3:1). We need to fix our thoughts on things above (Col 3:2), and on whatever is true, right, pure, lovely, admirable, excellent and praiseworthy (Phil 4:8) in order to bring refreshing and to refocus on truth. The disciplines of silence and solitude can be powerfully restorative, giving our minds time to recover and to restore balance after the relentlessly frantic pace of modern life. The disciplines of the mind are far from irrelevant: given the intellectual sewage through which we daily wade, they are indispensable to healthy living.

Simplicity and sacrifice

I have argued throughout this book that to be truly contagious we need firstly to be transformed inwardly to such a degree that it is outwardly visible, so that we're so full of life that we provoke a response. Secondly, we need to break into people groups that are as yet barely reached, such as the poor, the ethnic minorities, and the inner-city communities.

But we cannot have an impact on the inner city by remote control from middle-class suburbia. We have to face the challenge of finding Christians willing to move into the inner-city areas and stay there. To be honest, it's not altogether an attractive choice: it means being willing to live in a smaller house; to be worse off financially perhaps; more anxious over schooling;

facing a greater risk of crime. We would probably find ourselves under more time pressure. In the inner city there is the pressure of living with other cultures, the greater exposure to homelessness, mental ill-health, noise and pollution; there is less countryside and more litter. Inner city life is, of course, not without considerable compensations, and when we're where God wants us to be we can live in contentment regardless. But the point is this: if our Christian values go only skin deep and below that we're actually living for comfort, we'll not be equipped to make that choice. To be equipped, we will need to be engaged in the disciplines of service, sacrifice and simplicity. Such disciplines have never been more needed, if we're to see the Kingdom extended across our nation.

SUMMARY

Much of our increase in Christlikeness is worked out in a corporate context, but this does not diminish the importance of taking personal responsibility. Spiritual disciplines have been seen historically as central to growth. Although there are signs of change, Christians have, on the whole, under-utilised the disciplines for a variety of reasons. Nevertheless spiritual disciplines are inescapably biblical. A healthy approach is to see them as means and not ends; powerful tools that equip us for loving God and loving people. Far from being irrelevant, the discipline of our thinking is essential in an age when we are bombarded by so much that seeks to shape us. And far from being introspective, practising the disciplines of sacrifice, service and simplicity are essential if we are to see breakthroughs in the inner city.

Chapter 6

BE FILLED!

Measles. If I've got them, there's a chance I'll give them to someone else. Likewise, the more we're filled with God, the more likely it is that we will touch others with His love: we become contagious with life.

Living in constant intimacy with Him, we become both more available for change, more malleable, more easily worked into the likeness of Christ.

Living in constant togetherness with our loving Father, interacting, giving and receiving, fills us with joy, security and celebration. This is both visible and desirable to those around us: we become *contagious in who we are*.

Living in constant communication with God, constantly hearing His voice, allows us to imitate Jesus by walking aligned with the will of the Father, doing only what the Father instructs. In this way we become *dangerous to the world in what we do*.

The question is 'How?' Most Christians, like myself, have been taught the goal, but have been given little idea of how to work towards it. My aim in this chapter is to explore some tools that start to address this need.

The focus of revelation

Our starting point has to be this: God makes Himself known! But what does He reveal? Here it's important that we have a healthy balance. So often we slip into the habit of thinking that God's revelation is focused on me: I want to hear from God because I want the answers to my questions, to have my needs met, problems solved, decisions made easier. But God isn't there to meet our needs; we're here to glorify Him. We know that God has always been a God of revelation, even before we were created, because He is unchanging. His revelation then is primarily about Himself. His very nature is to express His glory, His happiness, to celebrate His goodness, purity, power, creativity and love. The main focus of our communion with God is learning how to worship, to stand in awe of our wondrous Heavenly Father. We live in an age that gives scant regard to awe; it's something we as God's people need to cultivate.

But God is not a God who is far off. The other focus of His revelation is towards us, His children, to declare His presence, to proclaim His love! His intention has always been for us to share in His joy (1 Tim 4:4, 1 Tim 6:17), to grow and mature in our relationship with Him.

The problem

The Fall had cataclysmic effects on humanity. Adam and Eve hid; they could no longer bear the presence of God. Fallen human beings are so damaged that they have become too fragile to handle the revelation of God as it was intended; it's simply too overwhelming. We see many references to this in Scripture:

- 1 Tim 6:16 says that God dwells in light which is 'unapproachable';
- Exodus records the people's terror when God and Moses meet on Sinai;

- Daniel's encounters with God left him devastated, and physically exhausted (Dan 8: 27; Dan 10: 8–10);
- Isaiah likewise was stunned by his experience of God (Isaiah 6: 5) and Jeremiah described His word as like a fire, a hammer that shatters rocks (Jer 23:29).

Perhaps, and this is only speculation, the hardening of men's hearts was not only a result of living separated from the fullness of God's love, but a matter of self-defence against the overwhelming power of His revelation.

God's solution

The Fall and the subsequent hardening of men's hearts have no doubt dulled our capacity to receive God's revelation, but I also suspect that it's out of His mercy, recognising our weakness, that God has made Himself invisible to us, and graciously lowered His voice to a whisper. This is why most people, especially those who are not Christians, are only dimly aware of Him.

Imagine for a moment that we're playing a game: the objective is to get to know someone, but we're not allowed to meet him or her face to face. How would we go about it? A good idea would be to talk to them indirectly, over the phone. Perhaps we could find out what they have done, to learn from their actions. Maybe we could read things they've written, or look at things they've made. We could ask other people what they know. We could learn things by going to where they live and looking at their belongings. Perhaps if they were close by we could see their footprints, their shadow, feel their heat.

Knowing God can be analogous to this, only it's not so much a game as an exciting adventure! God has written the Scriptures to reveal Himself, and these also tell of His deeds and actions. We can listen to the testimony of others, both alive now and throughout history to learn more about Him. We can pray, talking to Him and listening to His voice. In our own spirit we can sense His presence; and although we can't see Him directly we see 'a poor reflection as in a mirror' (1 Cor 13:12). The Bible tells us that God reveals Himself powerfully through what He has made, through creation 'For since the creation of the world God's invisible qualities – His eternal power and divine nature – have been clearly seen, being understood from what has been made' (Rom 1:20). Ultimately and supremely He revealed Himself when He came to dwell on the earth, clothed (fortunately for those alive at the time) in human form.

There is no doubt that God longs for intimacy with His children, and delights in it when it occurs. The full restoration of humanity to this level of relationship is one of His most cherished dreams, a prospect He exults in! Throughout the Scriptures analogies of father and son, bride and groom emphasise this dimension of God's plan. The problem certainly isn't that there's a shortage of revelation from God.

It's amazing to think that all around us the air is full of TV waves, radio signals, and satellite phone messages. They're completely invisible, but if we have the appropriate equipment, know how to use it and how to tune the aerials we can receive astonishing communications, and indeed send our own messages around the world. As children of God, we have a deep passion to know Him more, and we know that His revelation is all around us. As new creations we have the equipment to receive it and respond to it. It's a question of learning to 'tune-in'.

Designed for intimacy with God

God created Adam and Eve specifically for an intimate relationship with Him. I believe that *every* aspect of our design reflects this. Far too often we assume that our means of connecting with God is limited to our spirit and our mind. But what about all the other aspects of our human make-up?

Let's look at what it is to be a human being, and how all our faculties can be directed towards receiving His revelation and responding to it.

Our senses

Humans have amazing senses, which give us an incredible capacity to interact with Creation. It's no accident that food tastes good! We're not simply driven to eat by the need to survive, we can enjoy and celebrate what God has provided for us. We can hear beautiful sounds, experience different textures, enjoy a warm fire on a cold day, cool water when it's summer. We can delight in the scent of flowers. We can watch the clouds or a sunset. The point is that we have the capacity in our senses to exult in the creation, in order to glorify the Creator. We are reminded of His presence everywhere. We see some of His qualities reflected in what He has made, and are prompted to worship Him.

Our aesthetic and creative capability

There are over one million species on the earth, of which no less than 3,700 are mammals. Only one species has art galleries. God gave us the amazing gift of aesthetic awareness so that we can comprehend His beauty. Not only this, He gave us the capacity to be creative, to produce beautiful things that glorify Him. Even though we are fallen we still have this capacity to produce works of art, and fine design. These, shadows though they may be, can reveal something of the beauty of God, if we choose to look for it.

Our capacity for reason

God has given us the capacity for reason, reflection, analysis and synthesis. The Bible refers to the mind, but also speaks of the thought of our hearts. Our thinking is often involved when we are using our other faculties, and is vital in receiving revelation from God through Scripture, prophecy and ideas.

Our bodies

Eric Liddell is quoted in the film *Chariots of Fire* as saying 'When I run, I feel His pleasure'. Our bodies, so often despised by Christian tradition, are an amazing gift from God. Our activities and posture have spiritual dimensions. In the Bible we see many examples of this: David dancing before the Lord, Moses' arms held aloft to see the battle won. It's important not to underestimate the importance of different postures when we pray: when we kneel, or lie prostrate, or stand with our arms raised we will tend to hear different things and say different things to God. It's interesting to note that what we think of as the Muslim praying position, face to the ground, a posture of such humility, was very probably copied from the early Christians. C S Lewis, in his *Screwtape Letters*[1], refers to the importance of our posture when praying. We all know what a difference it can make to worship when people stand and raise their arms, or sit with arms folded. Sometimes we need to change the angle of an aerial to get better reception!

Our emotions

Western Christianity, for so long emphasising the intellectual, has tended to be suspicious of emotions. To reject the role of our emotions because of the danger of emotionalism is to throw out the baby with the bath water. We need to recognise that our emotions are a gift from God, designed to receive revelation of God's passions. Engaging our emotions helps us to take off our blinkers and read the Bible afresh. We discover there a God who is profoundly passionate, who freely and fully expresses sorrow, anger, love, jealousy, indignation, joy, and compassion. British culture is famously repressive of emotions: we fear losing control; fear vulnerability from revealing our feelings; we are embarrassed to affect others by expressing ourselves. God has no such inhibitions, no stiff upper lip. He does not need to fear losing control or being vulnerable; and He certainly wants to affect people.

Our moral awareness

Humans have a capacity to understand right and wrong, to be morally aware. Alone, of all the creatures on the Earth, we have judicial systems and penal codes based on ethical values. This too is a faculty given by God for communion with Him, for by it we have the ability to appreciate and respond to His awesome purity, holiness and righteousness.

Our imagination

We have the capacity to imagine, to see things in our minds that are not simply observed in the physical world. We have dreams. Why do we have these abilities? Perhaps to see things before they happen is part of the mechanics of faith, through which we know God. Perhaps this ability is to give us a taste of the freedom of the new heaven and new earth, and to rejoice in it. Maybe it reminds us that 'with God all things are possible'? Again, the imagination is an area that is treated with suspicion by many Christians. My answer is the same: yes, in a fallen world, any of the gifts of God, including our minds, including the Scriptures themselves can be abused (we have only to think of the cults), but this doesn't mean that we should discard them. Rather, with God's help and direction we are to learn how to use them properly. Let's not surrender any of our inheritance!

Non-verbal communication

Research indicates that non-verbal signals play a key role in human communication. It's one of the reasons why people remember more by attending a sermon than listening on tape or reading a transcript. These non-verbal signals are often in the form of body language, but can also include tone of voice, the effect of pauses and so on. Although the Bible says that God is Spirit, it nevertheless makes references to Him in physical terms: His outstretched arm, the hand of God, His back,

His face, His voice. Is it possible that we have the ability somehow to read God's body language? Can we learn to sense his arms reaching out to hold us, to sense His stance as He protects His people, to sense a raised eyebrow of amusement and delight?

Sense of humour

Our capacity for humour sets people apart from other creatures. I believe the ability to laugh is part of our God-given capacity to share in His joy and celebration. It is part of our ability to rejoice in the fullness of life of which He is the author.

Our will

God has given us the capacity to make choices: we are not mere biological automatons driven purely by instincts. This faculty is highly significant in many respects, as it enables us to share in the purposes of God, to be partners in the family business. But our wills also give us the capacity to appreciate God's will, to understand His plans, to delight in the fact that every perfect act of God is consciously willed by Him: nothing is by accident or default. It brings us to a fresh revelation of the goodness of God.

Memory

The importance of remembrance is stressed throughout the Bible; the Passover and the other festivals were all instituted to bring to remembrance the mighty deeds of God. Jesus called His disciples to break bread and drink wine in remembrance. Our capacity to remember the works of God in Bible times, throughout Church history and in our own life prompts us to give thanks, to honour his power and faithfulness. Our ability to remember God's previous interactions with us gives roots to our relationship with Him.

Putting it into practice

In my own church we're developing practical exercises, some of which aim to teach us how to use all our faculties in our inter-action with God. Others are aimed at developing a sense of awe. They're all about growing in intimacy with God. Here are some examples that we've used on weekend retreats.

Learning to see

For this exercise I use a metal kitchen sieve, which I place on a coffee table in the centre of the group. It doesn't have to be a kitchen sieve, but using something that is entirely mundane and everyday is relevant. Then we begin to explore different ways of 'seeing' the sieve, and using them to engage with God in some way. Here are some of the thoughts that emerged from our last group:

- We can see the substance, the metal of the sieve, and reflect on the way that it is made up of countless atoms, themselves composed of mind boggling particles doing extraordinary things. (We had a scientist in the group, who told us some amazing things about matter.) This became a vehicle to worship the God who 'holds all things together' (Col 1:17).
- We can focus instead on the light reflected off the surface, a unique pattern to every person in the room, changing with even the tiniest shift of viewpoint, and allow ourselves to reflect on God's light.
- We can look at the holes, the spaces between the substance. We're trained to look at what 'is' and rarely think to look at what 'is not'. My wife, an architect, has taught me a great deal about looking at the beauty of spaces. In a similar vein we can focus on the sieve in its context, and see how it relates to the things around it.
- We can use our imagination to explore what the sieve would look like from above, below, from inside, looking out at our faces peering in! It's incredible to reflect on the completeness

and consistency of the Creation: there are flowers growing where no one will see them, beautiful views that are never appreciated.

- We can see historically, reflecting on the history of the sieve, the story of its formation, its journey to us beginning from a piece of ore in a rock, and the number of people who have been involved in that journey. God is the God of history. He knows every detail of the history of everything. He knows our history, indeed we were predestined before the creation of the world.

- We can see biblically, being reminded of when Jesus reveals to Peter that Satan desired to sift him like wheat, but that He had prayed for Peter (Luke 22:31).

- We can see prophetically: a sieve is designed to let some things through but not others. Do we keep out the right things? Do we filter out things we should let through?

We send everyone in the group off for half an hour by themselves to practice 'seeing', and later in the weekend we give opportunity for feedback for those who wish to do so. The key point about the exercise is that it's something we can do when we return home as part of our everyday life. The whole focus of the weekend is not to escape 'normal life' for a couple of days, but rather to learn tools that will help us to live 'real life' in the midst of our ordinary daily activities.

That's why we use a kitchen sieve: it's to reinforce the idea that we can use whatever is around us to help us become more aware of His presence, to help people break out of the spiritual/secular divide in their thinking. This is probably the main challenge of the weekend, helping people to break out of their preconceptions, to give them permission and confidence to explore their relationship with the God. It's about realising that God is Lord over all, present, available, loving us and revealing Himself to us whether we're washing up, playing football, putting the kids to bed, buying new wiper blades, or sitting in a meeting.

Developing our sense of wonder

Contrary to the practice of other religious leaders of the time, Jesus welcomed the attention of children. He taught that we should become like children in order to see the Kingdom of God. I'm sure there are many layers to this, but perhaps one of the most significant is the capacity children have for awe and wonder. They see the world about them without the contempt bred by familiarity. They are excited and impressed by what they see, and have a capacity to rejoice that is enviably uncomplicated. As adults, especially in our culture, we are too busy and too superior to give much time to wonder. If we're to rediscover our capacity to wonder, to add this marvellous dimension to our worship, we may need to practice. Here are some practical exercises that some people have found helpful.

Contemplating the infinite and the eternal

It's a commonplace remark that 'We can't possibly grasp the infinite and the eternal'. I think we need to challenge this. After all, we are designed with eternity in mind, to live forever with Him! I'm sure we can learn to appreciate a lot more if we make an effort.

Infinite dimensions of each moment. Imagine you're in the new heaven and new earth. You decide you'd like to explore with God one particular second of your life. You could re-live what you were doing, thinking and feeling at that moment. You could see what it was like to be any one of another 5 billion people alive at that same second. You could ask God to show you what any one of those people was experiencing. You could zoom in and see the world from an infinite number of viewpoints. You could have a guided tour of how the rays of light were configured. Or you could zoom out and see what trends in the world were being influenced by your action at that moment; or see the impact if you had done something different. Each moment of your life is infinitely complex. God encompasses all of this! Allow yourself to be filled with awe and wonder.

The new heavens and earth. By and large we live our lives assuming that the next day will come. Perhaps our eternal life is like that, lived each day at a time, getting up with wonderful things to look forward to! As you go through your day, keep asking yourself: 'How would this look if it were a day in the new earth?' What are you looking forward to doing? What are you longing to being free of? Allow God to fill you with wonder and joyous anticipation of your future in Him.

Latent capabilities. No doubt many of our capabilities that have been damaged and lost since the Fall will be restored. Allow yourself to ponder what these latent capabilities might be. Perhaps we'll be able to communicate with animals (presumably Adam had some way of ruling them). How extraordinary that would be! Revelation 2:26 refers to ruling over nations: how will that feel? God asks Job if he has ever commanded the morning or caused the dawn to know its place (Job 38:12). Given the chance, how would we do it? Even as fallen humanity we have a tremendous ability to extend ourselves through tools, cars, phones etc. What will this capability look like when fully restored in the new heavens and earth?

The wonder of creation

The Bible says that creation declares the greatness of God (Ps 19), and Job 38–42 describes how God uses His creation to fill Job with a sense of wonder and humility. Find a place where you are surrounded by nature: ideally out in the countryside, or otherwise your garden, or a park. Spend time appreciating the wonder of nature. Close your eyes and see how many sounds you can hear; you'll probably find that your mind is trained to filter many of them out, so it takes practice to notice them all. Look closely at flowers, leaves, twigs, see the beauty with which they are made. Touch things, feel the texture; smell things. Spend some time looking at the clouds, always changing. Watch the beauty of a sunset and consider that from God's point of view sunrise and sunset don't stop, they move continuously around the world as it turns. In all these things, give thanks to God!

God's people

The Bible says that people are the climax of His creation. Yet so often we take people for granted. If we live in a city, we might see more people in a couple of hours than someone in the middle ages would have seen in a lifetime. It's easy to treat people as objects. Here are some simple ideas to help us think about people in a fresh way.

All people are real. Find a place where you can sit and simply observe people you don't know: a park bench, a railway station. Practice looking at people while listening to God. Hear His love and pride in what He has made. Every one of them has trillions of synapses in their brains, and capabilities that are far beyond the most powerful computer. They have miles of veins and arteries, and a gut with the surface area of a tennis court! They are fearfully and wonderfully made. God made them and loves them enough to keep them in existence. Think about each person's uniqueness: every one has a unique blend of gifts, abilities, experiences, memories, ideas, beliefs. Each one has a unique history of scars from living in a fallen world. God loves each one of them.

The connections game. Contemplate all the people to whom you are connected by a simple object such as a hammer! The man who sold it to you, the lorry driver who brought it to him, the sales clerk who made the invoice, the doctor who cared for him, the car mechanic who mended the doctor's car, the person who made her overalls etc. How many people's lives will you touch today without realising? God knows every connection of this incredible web of relationships in which we live every day.

Six steps to the world! How many people do you know, either closely or as acquaintances? It's probably over a hundred. Let's take 50. Each of those 50 have a circle of 100 people. There may be an overlap with the people you know, so let's say they know another 50 people that you don't. Each of these 50 knows another 50 new people, and so on. In just six steps you have connections to 15.5 *billion* people. That's three times the world's population! If we can have a contagious effect on those we know . . .

Conclusion

As we begin to take hold of these ideas and *practise* them, we find ourselves living more and more in touch with Him. The quality of our lives is transformed: that which seemed pointless and futile becomes alive with potential; we find ourselves more joyful, more peaceful. We enjoy life more. We find that our motives change, and things that were a drudge become an act of love. We find that God speaks to us in ways we never expected, and that we change more readily. We find that we're more sensitive to God's leading, we're more alive to ways of showing His love to others. We start to see the potential we have to be the bearer of the blessing of God wherever we go in the world. We become more contagious.

SUMMARY

God is a God of revelation. Primarily He reveals His own glory, but He also reveals His infinite love to humanity. We were designed to live in constant intimate communion with God. The Fall had disastrous effects, creating a terrible separation. It also left human beings so weakened and fragile that God's full revelation would be overwhelming. But God found a huge range of dif-

ferent ways of revealing Himself to us nevertheless. As
Christians, we have an incredible new capacity for relationship
with Him. This is something we need to practise and work at
because we're living in a fallen world, and still putting off the old
nature. God designed every aspect of our humanity for relationship with Him. We can learn, by simple exercises to use our
minds, bodies, emotions, aesthetic awareness, imagination etc.
to engage with the living God. As we do so we find that we can
live in communion with Him in every moment of our lives
regardless of how mundane or 'unspiritual' our activities may
seem. In this way we find our lives becoming more abundant: we
rejoice in the Lord always, we pray without ceasing. We become
good news wherever we go: we are more contagious because
our lives are more attractive.

Chapter 7

MODELS AND MEANS

'It's not what you know . . . but who you know', they say. And this is surely true for Christians. However, for at least a century the church's main strategy has been to pump congregations full of knowledge through the medium of the sermon. But knowledge isn't enough: to make contagious Christians we need to break out and look at ways of building in the character and the lifestyle of Jesus. And to rely exclusively on the sermon is to neglect half of the tools in the toolbox. Let's have a look at the range of equipment that the Bible offers us.

Dimensions

People are extremely complex. Not only that, they work differently over a period of time. And each one is unique. So, in exploring ways to help people change, we might expect to find a diversity of means. In the Bible that's precisely what we do find, a number of dimensions:

Knowledge. Jesus gave himself extensively to the impartation of knowledge and understanding by teaching large numbers of people. We see this in His Sermons on the Mount and on the Plain, and in His teaching in synagogues. Sometimes His teaching was direct, at other times He used parables. He clearly wanted His followers to 'know' many things, ranging from the practicalities of living God's way daily, to awesome revelation about judgement and eternal life. His emphasis was always on grasping spiritual truth, rather than simply communicating information.

Discovery. Jesus encouraged His disciples to learn through discovery. The New Testament records many occasions where the twelve questioned Him privately for further insight into His parables or sayings. He frequently allowed others, for example Nicodemus, (John 3) to initiate the conversation, to ask questions. Through guided dialogue, Jesus helped people to grow in revelation.

Confrontation. Uncomfortable though it may be for us, Jesus often used loving confrontation to help people break through to a new place of understanding or commitment. Examples include the rich young ruler (Matt 19), Jesus' instruction to let the dead bury their own dead (Matt 8), and His frequent encounters with the Pharisees. It's easy to downplay Jesus' use of challenge, particularly because most leaders find it stressful and difficult to apply appropriately, but it's not something we should walk away from.

Experience. I think there can be little doubt that direct experience, encountering the works of Jesus, brought about significant changes in His disciples. Jesus' calming of the storm evoked an immediate response of awe and worship, and seeing Lazarus raised is likely to have made a profound impression (John 11:45).

Action. Jesus used practical hands-on activity as a key feature of His disciple-making. The disciples were more than merely by-standers. Jesus engaged them in the feeding of the five thousand (Luke 9:14–17), sent out the seventy-two in pairs into the mission field, and supported them as they prayed for the sick and demon-possessed (Matt 17:15–20). We need to recognise that disciple-making is in part a *physical* activity. It's easy to fall into the trap of assuming discipleship is a cerebral and inward process, and fail to appreciate the vital role our bodies play.

Power and prayer. Significant change was effected in the disciples by the outpouring of the Holy Spirit at Pentecost (Acts 2); and Paul refers to Timothy's gift, imparted by the laying on of hands (2 Tim 1:6). Paul encourages the Ephesians to be continually filled with the Spirit (Eph 5:18). Through prayer, and God's response to those prayers, Paul expects the Ephesians to have 'the eyes of their heart enlightened' (Eph 3:18), and the Philippians to 'abound in love' (Phil 1:9). The Apostles prayed that God would give them boldness to proclaim the Gospel more clearly, and power to demonstrate it (Acts 4:29–30).

Crisis. This is perhaps the dimension we least like to contemplate, yet the Scriptures are clear that God will often use the crises that we encounter as opportunities to take us into greater maturity. It's only in the crisis that we truly understand God's absolute power to 'work all things together for good'. (Romans 8:28). We're reminded often (e.g. 1 Pet 1:6, Romans 5:3–4) that suffering and trials are used by God to develop our character. We live in a society that steers unswervingly for the comfort zone and regards problems and trials in an essentially negative light. Learning to change our response, to see the potential in difficult situations for God to change and strengthen us, is a key for growth. And it can certainly make disciples stand out from the crowd, with a contagiously alternative lifestyle.

I think it's readily apparent that we need the diversity of models we see in the New Testament because no one of them can encompass the range of dimensions we see here.

Using the models

From-the-front teaching

Biblical examples would be Jesus' Sermon on the Mount, Peter's Pentecost sermon, and Paul's letters being read out to the early churches.

Teaching, especially the sermon, has the seat of honour in many churches. More than that, it's often the only seat at the table and is expected to accomplish everything required for growing disciples. I'm not arguing against the sermon, rather that we should take a fresh look at what it is best suited for, and to see it as part of a much bigger canvas of options open to us.

The sermon is particularly well suited to transmitting knowledge. But it's generally much less good at giving an experience, and rarely has a direct hands-on element in the terms I've described above. There's usually little scope for discovery through dialogue, because a sermon is essentially one-way communication. The sermon may have a confrontational element although this will tend to strike home for some of the listeners and not others. It is arguably ideal for communicating doctrine, where clarity of thought is essential. But it's much less suited to developing qualities, which often emerge through experience, or to developing skills which need input tailored very specifically to the needs and character of individual disciples. As a tool, it doesn't readily lend itself to personal accountability: that is, disciples being held to account for applying what they've learned.

There are other forms of teaching which address some of these issues. Students at Bible colleges, training with para-church organisations, or engaged in distant learning programmes for example, are expected to engage in dialogue, and to discover for themselves. They're much more closely held to account for what they've learned than is typical for most members of congregations.

There's another reason for us to look afresh at from-the-front teaching in our churches. Sermons have tended to reflect the values of our Western culture in being orientated towards the faculties of the left side of the brain: logical, sequential, verbal, analytical and abstract. We need more balance in our teaching, to draw more on the faculties of the right side of our brain: visual, associative, concrete, specific, application orientated, synthesis. This is a matter of urgency, for three reasons. Firstly, if we are to have any hope of reaching the poor, we need to recognise that non-book culture is more right-brained; secondly, amongst the educated too there is a move towards a more right-brained approach due to the influence of television, computers and the Internet. Thirdly, Jesus commonly preached this way: the Gospels reveal a teaching style that makes frequent use of story telling, everyday practical illustrations, visual aids and humour. I'll return to this later.

Small group

Jesus made extensive use of this model, spending three years with His twelve disciples. Interestingly Jesus appears to have had an inner circle of three, Peter, James and John, within the twelve. Paul usually travelled with a group of companions on his missionary journeys.

Small groups were vital in the Wesleyan revival and have probably been one of the key rediscoveries in recent years, whatever form they take. Their intimacy can prove ideal for dialogue and discovery, for working through application at a personal level, for maintaining greater accountability, as a place for prayer and laying on of hands. The dangers of small groups are familiar territory to most church leaders: intimacy can decay towards introversion; acceptance can quickly become cosy and without challenge; unity can tend towards exclusivity; and subtle power struggles emerge. Some churches are finding that switching from groups focused on one particular function/ministry/activity, in favour of the multi-functional cell model has helped resist these tendencies. Others are finding single sex groups effective, drawing on the experience of churches in Argentina and the 'Promise Keepers' in the USA.

One-to-one

The Bible indicates that people can be changed through the experience of rubbing shoulders with someone else over a period of time. A process of impartation takes place. Biblical examples would include Jesus' special relationship with Peter; Paul's relationship with Barnabas, and later Timothy. The principle is well summed up in the Proverbs: 'He who walks with the wise grows wise' (13:20).

More recently this model experienced something of a revival in the 1970's and 80's in the 'shepherding movement'. It's influence was relatively short lived, because of the storm of reaction to 'heavy shepherding' abuses, both actual and imagined. This model does indeed carry the risk of unhealthy control, but the response needn't be to reject it. Rather we should adopt the biblical safeguard of setting boundaries to ensure that we disciple people to Jesus, not to ourselves (1 Cor 1:12–13). It is true that Paul encouraged people to imitate himself and other godly men, but it's clear that this applies to their Christ-like qualities (1 Cor 4:16–17; Heb 13:7; Heb 6:12).

There are other risks too: those chosen may become arrogant, seeing themselves as an elite, and those not selected may become resentful. There's a danger of signalling growth to maturity as an optional extra for the 'spiritual high fliers'. As a model, it can be very labour intensive especially for leaders. And there's the problem of 'quality control'. The biblical model is to walk with the wise: we all know what happens when the blind lead the blind.

These are real issues, but it's important not to overreact against what is clearly a valuable, biblical model. The key is not to use the one-to-one model exclusively, but to balance it with other tools involving all church members in a wider strategy. To use it exclusively would be inconsistent with the biblical model of the Church as a body where all the parts are valuable and essential. Risks there may be, but they are risks that Jesus and Paul were prepared to take.

One-to-one discipling is particularly effective in the context of apprenticeship, where a disciple is seeking to grow in a specific ministry, by working alongside someone with more experience in that particular gifting. Apprenticeship of this sort is a long-term investment: very counter-cultural in the age of the quick fix.

Pairs

When Jesus sent out the twelve (Mark 6), and the seventy-two (Luke 10) to preach and demonstrate the Kingdom of God in power, He sent them in pairs.

'As iron sharpens iron, so one man sharpens another' (Proverbs 27:17). Although many churches make use of prayer partnerships, which may be pairs or more often triplets, it's much less common to see church members sent out in pairs for proclamation and power ministry in the way that the early disciples were. Working as a pair provides mutual support and encouragement, allows a variety of gifts to be expressed, and leaves no place to hide! The Scriptures suggest that it was very effective in building the disciples' confidence, even to the point that Jesus felt it necessary to deflate them somewhat (Luke 10:17–21).

Spiritual retreats

I've referred in the previous chapter to the importance of spiritual disciplines to Jesus and the early church. Sometimes these disciplines are best pursued in times of withdrawal. There are over twenty references in the Gospels to Jesus' habit of withdrawing to lonely places. Sometimes Jesus withdrew alone, and at other times with His disciples. For inner-city congregations in particular, the retreat gives an invaluable opportunity to slow down, clear the mind and refocus on priorities. It also allows new spiritual skills to be learned, practised and partially established before they're tested 'on the battlefield'.

Apostles, prophets and evangelists

Making dangerous disciples is more than a question of looking at what we do and the way we do it. *Who* does it is a vital consideration. Most UK churches have leadership structures that are heavily weighted towards pastors and teachers. Whatever strategy we develop in our churches, we will need to find ways of incorporating the other ministries identified in Ephesians 4. Their specific purpose is to prepare, build up, and bring to maturity the people of God (vv 12–13). Indeed, Ephesians 2:20 refers to the role of the apostolic and prophetic ministries as foundational. This is not to devalue the pastoral and teaching ministries, but it seems clear that all of the ministries are designed to work together, to complement each other, and maintain balance. Without the contribution of the apostolic, prophetic and evangelistic ministries, there's a much greater risk that our churches will lose vision; the sense of purpose and calling becomes blurred. If we lose this sharpness, we default quickly towards introversion and maintenance mentality. These other ministries are often uncomfortable to pastors. They can appear disruptive, but we need their gifts to help us retain our radical edge, to push the boundaries, to take our contagiousness to where it is needed: out in the world.

Conclusions

Most of us, Church leaders and congregations alike, tend to focus on the methods we enjoy, feel we know something about, and feel comfortable with. It can be daunting to recognise, perhaps, that there are a number of models and dimensions that we rarely use, and which are less familiar. But if we're to see our churches filled with dangerous disciples, explore we must. We may feel that we lack gifting in some of these areas. We may feel insecure at first. We will progress, hopefully, to a recognition that God has planted people across the churches with a wide range of gifts and experience, and that others have what we lack. This is certainly a New Testament pattern, where we see Peter and John supporting Philip in Samaria (Acts 8); and Paul planting, Apollos watering in Corinth (1 Cor 3:6).

We need the capacity to learn humbly from other streams, denominations and traditions, learning from their wisdom, and from their mistakes. This process will encourage us out of our self-sufficiency, into a much greater understanding of our inter-dependence, a new honouring of the whole body of Christ. An exciting result!

SUMMARY

Making contagious Christians requires us to work in a number of different dimensions that we can see demonstrated in the New Testament. As well as imparting knowledge, we'll need to recognise that discovery, confrontation, experience, action, power, prayer, and crisis are all important to the process of helping people grow into the likeness of Christ. To make use of these dimensions, we may need to re-evaluate the models we currently use. The Bible shows us a number of options: teaching from the front, small groups, one-to-one, pairs, retreats. The key is to find the most effective ways of using these resources. Reviewing all our options in this way, we may feel that there are many new areas to explore, and much that we can learn from others across the wider body of Christ. Whatever the strategy, the Scriptures challenge us to include the Ephesians 4 ministries, which are vital for ensuring our disciple-making retains its cutting edge. In our aim to fill our churches with dangerous dis-ciples, we can't afford not to use all the options God has made available to us as skilfully as we can.

Chapter 8

LEARNING KEYS

What we actually *say* is one thing. But people act on what they *receive*. Certainly, making contagious Christians means shaking up both what we say and how we say it, checking out our 'delivery systems'. This is the side that church leaders look at. But equally important is the other side of the coin: looking at all those factors that influence how we learn, that help us to change most effectively.

Environment

It is easy to fall into 'church-think', focusing our attention on church activities, church meetings, and church structures, especially for leaders working full time. But while church activities are important in themselves, they mustn't become our sole aim. Living as disciples, *being* church, takes place primarily in the 95 per cent of our lives which happens outside church meetings. Over recent years we've seen changes in this regard: many churches have taken the significant step of recognising that discipling doesn't only take place in a church building on a Sunday morning. Through house groups and cell groups, we've at least made it as far as the home! And we're also seeing changes in how we perceive the role of church: it's not so much that members exist for the benefit of the church, rather that church is a resource for disciples. One of the purposes in meeting together is to receive encouragement, support and healing of the wounds we've received out in the world.

So far, so good. But I think we need to go further. The home is still a relatively safe environment. And to see church as a place of refuge, a place for licking wounds, is too passive: we need to be prepared to go on the offensive. We need to take a radical look at discipling 'out there' on the front line where people are living out their lives, the place where they meet most of their not-yet-Christian friends, especially the workplace. Most church leaders attend conferences with the laudable aim of learning things that they will pass on to their flock; some travel overseas to experience first hand what God is doing there, with the aim of imparting it on their return. Yet the sad fact is that most leaders rarely visit their flock at their workplace. Surely we can see God in action there too? Isn't it likely that our teaching, support and discipling will be far more relevant when we truly understand the pressures and challenges our members are facing, by seeing them first hand? Most church leaders have preached about living God's way all the time, in all aspects of our lives, instead of having a great divide between our 'normal' life and our 'spiritual' life. But we send completely the opposite message by never meeting with our members out there in the real world, and helping them to apply spiritual truth to the issues they face. It's interesting to note how much of Jesus' ministry took place on or beside the Sea of Galilee, the workplace for many of his listeners, including of course, several of his close disciples.

There's a challenge here to leaders. Why is it rare for leaders to meet with their flock in the workplace? Perhaps because it's time consuming, and we want quicker methods. Perhaps, if we're honest with ourselves, we find it less glamorous and exciting than a ministry trip overseas. Perhaps deep down we're afraid that we don't have the answers, and feel inadequate to help people with the messy situations they actually have to deal with.

I want to emphasise that I'm not simply arguing for more pastoral visits, or for those visits to include the workplace as well as the home. I'm talking about something deeper, a change in our understanding of church, which turns church *inside out*. We need to recognise the realities of modern lifestyles: professional people working longer and longer hours; shift workers whose availability is unpredictable and often inconvenient; single parents who are tied to the home unless they can have child care support. If leaders persist in the assumption that the onus is on the disciples to come to them for training, we either rule out many of the people whose lifestyles are incompatible with our church timetable or increase the pressures on them still further. We need a radical re-think that reverses this flow, which takes resources to people rather than vice versa. In doing so we also reinforce the idea that we are to be salt and light in the world rather than simply good church members[1].

Accountability

There's an adage that says: 'People don't do what you expect, but what you inspect.' Accountability is central to the discipling process. Jesus himself rendered account to the Father; the Seventy-two gave an account of themselves to Jesus when they returned from their mission; Paul monitored Timothy closely. The parable of the talents expresses the same idea. There are three keys to healthy accountability.

Firstly, we need to have sown a vision for its purpose, so that it's seen as a tool to help us grow, shed the old nature, become more like Jesus, living life to the full. Without this vision it quickly becomes a legalistic whip.

Secondly, accountability is a two-way channel. In one direction, change within people has deeper roots when they report on their progress and accept responsibility for their growth. In the other direction, it is equally vital that they receive advice, support and authority.

Thirdly, to be most effective, accountability needs to be based on goals that are practical and specific, and ideally includes a way of identifying progress. Because of our tendency to 'spiritualise', we can often make discipleship a matter of vague generalities, whereas the New Testament writers clearly expected to see changes in people that were concrete and observable. The idea of accountability is well established, indeed accepted without question in the workplace, or when we're studying; how much more valuable then is it in the context of learning to live as we're meant to live – to the full.

Patterns of growth

Sometimes we can see change and growth to maturity following a linear process, a series of stages. We're reminded of this in 1 John 2 which refers to children, young men, and then fathers in the faith. But it's not always so simple! Sometimes Christians grow in several directions simultaneously; sometimes they seem to have reached C before they've grasped B. Sometimes we think we've understood something, and then God takes us back over the same ground later but at a deeper level. Most of us have had the experience of re-discovering the most basic truths in a fresh way. The Holy Spirit always works according to his agenda, and it's not always tidy to our way of thinking. Our strategy must always be flexible enough for this.

Pacing

We need to recognise that transmission of information is relatively quick, but changing character and behaviour is often a much slower process. We may need to change our expectations of the speed of progress. A three-point sermon can be very effective in communicating ideas and principles quickly. But if we're aiming to change behaviour or shape character, three points is probably two points too many. We may need to work on one thing at a time. We may need to be patient enough to repeat things until they have sunk in, to support, encourage and hold accountable until we see change take place. In most churches, the pastor preaches on a new subject each Sunday. It's time to challenge this convention. If our aim is to see people changed by what we teach, it makes more sense to preach on the same area until it has been grasped. With a typical teaching slot of half an hour per week, it's going to take some time for any message to get across. We're likely, naturally, to face some opposition from church members who see the pastor's job as being to create something new every week, and to whom the idea of actually being expected to change is something of a rude shock!

In a similar vein, church leaders often encourage their members to cover more ground in their Bible reading. At the risk of being controversial, I wonder sometimes if this is the right objective. Surely the aim is not to read more *per se*, but to be changed into His likeness. This might mean that we encourage people to read their Bibles *less* but truly digest and live out what they have read. If, for example, someone read only one verse a week, but diligently worked it into their life, and became changed by it, after a year they would have changed in fifty-two ways, no doubt delighting their leaders and impressing their not-yet-Christian friends! We may need to switch the emphasis from quantity to quality. It's a question again of keeping our eye on the objective, the end, and not the means.

Too many answers?

Many pastors and teachers would see, as a key objective of their teaching, the need to bring clarity, explanation and illumination. The aim is to help people understand a Bible passage or a doctrine by explaining the context, expanding the ideas, and perhaps using analogies and illustrations to give pointers on how to apply it. Central to this process is providing answers to the questions raised by the text or principle.

Intriguingly, when we look at Jesus we see that sometimes He uses a quite different approach. There are times when He communicates in ways that are difficult to understand: He spoke in parables, He spoke figuratively (John 16:25); even the Pharisees complained that He kept them in suspense and urged Him to speak plainly (John 10:24). On numerous occasions the disciples approached Him for further explanation of a parable. This reminds us that discipleship is not a passive process: our teaching needs to engage and stretch people, to help them grow. Posing questions and setting puzzles can be powerful tools for doing just this. Sometimes we learn more by wrestling with an issue than by spoon-feeding. By working through something for ourselves, we often find that we value the answer more, that the truth has put down deeper roots in us, and that we have a greater sense of ownership. I suspect that our tendency to concentrate on improving our delivery systems in churches, giving relatively little thought to how people learn, has seriously stunted the sense of ownership. It's very easy to fall in to the trap where disciple-making is something done *to* the congregation when in reality, as we've seen, we are all integrally part of the process.

To be honest, the pressure is always there for a leader to demonstrate knowledge and understanding. And then there's the appeal of the tidiness that comes from everyone having the same answers. Perhaps our members don't relish the idea of having to chew on the truth in order to digest it. But learning to live with loose ends is part of learning to live.

Out of print: the challenge of non-book culture

When I first began to think about helping my church members to become more contagious, I did the obvious thing: I visited a large Christian bookshop to buy a supply of suitable Bible study materials. Not just shelves but bookcases were full of material. But as I began to work my way through them I quickly realised that virtually all were written essentially for a middle-class, reasonably well educated, book-loving audience. My congregation is multi-racial: some have English as a second language; they live in an urban area; many of them are not well educated and don't particularly like reading. They are, to a significant degree, a non-book culture. The issue is not merely one of presentation, but about different ways of thinking. The materials I was looking at assumed thinking patterns based on abstract ideas; many in my congregation think in terms of practical concrete specifics. It wasn't 'Three keys to maturity (all beginning with the letter 'R') from the life of Zerubbabel' that was needed, so much as 'How I can help my neighbour on the housing estate cope with her violent husband'. I realised that excellent though all the materials were, it's pointless having great *delivery* systems, if people are unable to *receive* them. It dawned on me, with some horror, that I was going to have to produce my own materials, think for myself. . . .

On reflection, I realised that what I had found wasn't really surprising: it's simply a reflection of the predominantly middle-class culture of evangelical and charismatic churches. But it also reinforces that culture, and if we're not careful, may trap the church within it. If we're going to break out into other people groups, we need to find ways of communicating that they can receive. It's a challenge not only to our style, but also to the very way we think.

Left brain, right brain

The scientists tell us that the different parts of our brains perform different functions: our left hemisphere or left brain, controls our right hand and is the source of logical, verbal, sequential and abstract thought. The right brain thinks in visual terms, by association and in concrete specific ways.

Although of course everybody uses both parts of their brain, we're all different in the balance between these ways of thinking. This doesn't just apply to individuals: society as a whole can favour one or the other, and may shift over time.

Historically speaking Western culture was given a strong push towards left-brained thinking by the introduction of printing. Invented in the late 15th Century it developed into a communications revolution by the 17th Century. The sheer mechanics of reading, left to right, top to bottom, promoted left brain thinking. Following soon after, the scientific developments of the enlightenment followed by rationalism and then the industrial and scientific revolutions all reinforced the emphasis on reasoned logical forms of thinking. The church reflected these wider changes in society. Prior to the introduction of printing the medieval church used very different forms of communication: architecture whose scale and magnificence spoke of the glory and power of God, wall paintings and stained glass which related Bible stories, festivals and feast days, music and mystery plays. In other words, activities with strong right brain bias. In the printing revolution the Protestant church was a key player, even a driving force, seizing the opportunity afforded by print to promote new ideas. In subsequent centuries the Protestant church has reflected society's shift towards left-brain thinking patterns, with a strong emphasis on reading the Bible and on the primacy of the sermon. The methods used by the medieval church were largely sidelined. It's interesting that for most people outside the church, their expectation of a sermon is a boring talk with three points (all beginning with the same letter) in a logical sequence, with an emphasis on definitions and principles with little real connection to everyday life. This is a caricature, of course, but a revealing one.

For people that are disposed to these ways of thinking or to people who have been trained in an education system which emphasises the development of left brain thinking, well and good. Most middle-class people have received the benefit of this

kind of background and therefore find left brained communication patterns in our churches familiar. Indeed many would be
suspicious of any alternative, perhaps would not even perceive
that there are alternatives. However a large number of people do
not learn through these left-brain patterns of communication.
They learn more effectively in entirely different ways. Chris Key,
in his excellent work *Booked Out*[2] sets out some of the main
differences between book and non-book cultures and gives us
some very helpful pointers we need to explore.

Book people	Non-book people
Think in words.	Think in pictures.
Think in straight logical lines.	Think in patterns.
Store information in files and on computer disks.	Convert what is learned into memorable experiences.
Use watches, filofaxes and calendars.	Act when the time is right — or when the kids are ready.
Thinking is calm and cool.	Think in a way that is emotionally involved (hot).
Like to generalise.	Specific and concrete.
Like to learn alone.	Like to learn in groups.
Tend to take it all very seriously.	Like a laugh.
Continually search for new ideas.	Value traditions, customs, songs, proverbs, sayings . . .
Learn, but often fail to follow through.	Learn in order to do.
Collect books.	Collect badges, beer mats, ornaments.
Have lots of books at home.	Usually have a catalogue in the house.
Have book-lined studies.	Have workrooms (a corner for sewing, the garage for DIY).

(Quoted with permission)

If we are serious in our desire to reach out more effectively to other ethnic minorities and to the less well-educated sections of our society we need to take a radical look at how we communicate. This will mean exploring alternatives that make greater use of the visual, physical actions, story telling, participation, practical and specific application.

Exploring a non-book approach

In my own church we're trying tentatively to apply some non-book ideas in our prayer meetings. In our last half-night of prayer our first session was 'graffiti for the nation' – we gave everyone a can of spray paint or large marker pens and invited them to graffiti their prayers onto the wall (covered in lining paper). It was very interesting to see people who rarely pray in prayer circles suddenly released to express themselves. Some gained a new confidence that they could take part in prayer. Later in the same meeting when we came to break bread, we surrounded ourselves with an enclosing barrier of chairs. Each chair was labelled with the things that characterise fallen humanity, the chains that bind us: fear, rage, envy, addiction and so on. As we broke bread and drank wine, in pairs we gave thanks that Christ had broken each of these chains, and as we prayed we literally kicked over the chairs and 'broke out'. People rejoiced spontaneously, the impact was electrifying. When we were praying for not-yet-Christian friends, we wrote specific people's names onto boxes. Groups gathered around the boxes and each time someone prayed, we moved the box two carpet tiles forward until they all reached the cross, which we had erected at the front of the hall. It was interesting to see how some of the men, seeing other groups slightly ahead of them, discovered a new passion for evangelistic prayer!

Non-book evangelism

It's not just a question though of changing the way we do our meetings. We need to open our eyes to the evangelistic dimension. This point was brought home to me powerfully last year. One of our church members had been relationship-building with neighbours on a housing estate. Invitations to meetings had been ignored, offers to join an Alpha course rejected, social events avoided, leaflets thrown away. Three things *did* make an impact. Firstly, most of the church turned out for a sponsored walk to raise money for the playgroup on the estate. Secondly, on this walk, the Christian couples showed affection to each other, even though they had been married for years. Thirdly, the church member who was befriending them succeeded in her diet: she lost over five stones, and kept the weight off. She was able to do this because she was exploring the theology and ideas that I'm trying to communicate in this book: God dealt with the inner struggles that previously caused her to overeat and empowered her to diet by giving her a completely new motivation. She, and other church members were contagious in ways they never expected or were even aware of! I think there is a great deal for us all to learn here, and we'll learn more by stumbling forward than by standing still.

Resources

I referred earlier to my struggle to find materials suitable for non-book culture in a bookshop, which on reflection is none too surprising. The good news, however, is that a growing number of people are producing materials with this perspective, many of them working in churches located in urban priority areas. My respect for these groundbreaking pioneers is enormous. I've referred already to Chris Key's excellent work *Booked Out*; this was published by the Church Pastoral Aid Society (CPAS)[2] who are playing an invaluable role in linking up non-book culture initiatives. UNLOCK (formerly The Evangelical Urban Training Project)[3] is another goldmine of resources, both in terms of experienced advisers and a range of excellent small group materials for use in local churches. Finally, the Y Course[4] is a very exciting new initiative. This is a course aimed at people wanting to find out more about Christianity, but it has been designed specifically with post-modern, post-Christian culture in mind. It assumes no prior knowledge, deals with issues honestly, and uses many vivid contemporary illustrations to get points across effectively. It also emphasises that the goal is to be a disciple rather than a church-goer.

The visual revolution

I want to challenge a possible misconception: we'd be quite mistaken to think that non-book issues were relevant only to the urban poor or ethnic minorities. Parallel to the impact of printing centuries ago, our present age is witnessing a communications revolution. We are the first mass televisual generation. Given that in the UK the average person watches several hours of TV a day there can be little doubt that it's having a profound impact on our society. And now we're witnessing the computer revolution: already most schools make regular use of computer programmes and the Internet. The number of UK homes with personal computers is growing rapidly. What's significant here is that we have a generation using learning patterns that are radically different to what has gone before. The computer mouse certainly changes the order of things – the user is placed in complete control, setting the agenda, learning by exploring. They themselves determine the depth they wish to go to and the direction they wish to take. Both CD ROMS and the Internet are highly visual media using imagery, video clips and sounds, as well as purely text. By clicking with a computer mouse the computer user is not limited to learning about a subject in a logical sequential way but can jump sideways and backwards, building up a picture not by logical sequence, but by a series of associations.

This means that there are growing numbers of highly educated, highly qualified, well paid professionals who are working in essentially right-brain non-book ways. Looking at our society as a whole, we're in a state of flux. The issue here isn't simply about the number of books, sales of which remain healthy. Text-based and verbal communications will continue and so will left-brain thinking patterns. The point is that nevertheless our culture is experiencing a shift in favour of right-brain thinking. This has some profound implications for the church. Take the sermon for example: this is essentially a verbal medium, where the speaker both sets the agenda and then logically explores the subject. The congregation meanwhile, taking an essentially passive role, is expected to absorb the material over perhaps half an hour. This is a total contrast to the Internet user who is used to setting his own agenda, dwelling for a while on areas he doesn't understand, skipping things he is familiar with, working with sounds, images, thinking associatively and printing off the results when he has finished. We need to do some serious thinking about how to make use of new media as resources for discipling and about the impact that changes in learning styles may have on the way we work in our churches[5].

The death of the sermon?

Am I saying that the sermon is dead? Absolutely not! But we need to take a hard look firstly at what we preach and how we preach; and secondly at all the other available tools that we under-utilise at present.

The sermon is clearly a biblical model. It is also evident that Jesus' Sermon on the Mount was different in style from Peter's at Pentecost. Paul preached to the Corinthians 'without wise and persuasive words' (1 Cor 2:4) whereas reasoning was a central feature of his preaching in Athens. Peter's sermon at Pentecost drew on Old Testament Scripture; Paul's sermon in Athens began with references to Greek poets. In the Bible preaching adapted to the culture or circumstances and ours will need to do the same. But that is not to say that we should allow culture to set the agenda: it is absolutely critical that we resist the pressures of our age to 'dumb-down' the content of the sermon and to allow its style to degenerate to a fifteen-minute collection of sound bites. Sermons that are God-filled will always stretch and challenge; sermons that are words given by the Holy Spirit will engage people regardless of age, background or culture, and will do so far beyond their usual attention span. The challenge for leaders is to ensure that in content, style and anointing the sermon is all that it can be.

SUMMARY

If we're going to be effective at making Christians contagious, we need to look not only at what we're delivering, but how people best receive; we need to consider those factors which affect how people learn. This means breaking out of our cosy church meeting environment to support people on the front line of their lives. We will need to alter our expectations of the speed of change, and find ways of building in greater accountability. There are exciting challenges to face: adapting to non-book culture, and responding to the impact of TV, computers and the Internet on the way people think. We need to look afresh at the sermon in particular, to ensure that we're maximising its potential.

Chapter 9

A LOCAL CHURCH STRATEGY FOR DEVELOPING CONTAGIOUS CHRISTIANS

In the preceding chapters I have argued that we need to take a hard look at the way we're discipling people. But principles and ideas, no matter how appealing, are ultimately sterile unless we can apply them, find ways to weave them into the fabric of church life. This is a discipline in itself. It takes time, but then again, if discipling is central to our concept of church, what else should we be doing? Better to do the important things falteringly than the trivial things brilliantly. I've attempted to do this in my own church by setting out a strategy for making contagious Christians, which I've shown below. It's only illustrative, of course: each church is unique.

Aim

The aim is to outline a strategy for helping my congregation, including myself, to become more contagious. This involves identifying practical and achievable steps that will help us to be transformed more into the likeness Jesus, overflowing with fullness of life, with a radical impact on people and the society around us.

Background factors to consider

Size. The church is small in numbers. Just under 50 per cent of the congregation are from ethnic minorities. Some have been Christians for many years, while others are less experienced. About 15 per cent have special needs, including four that are blind or partially sighted. Some are single parents, one has a child with special needs. Some of the congregation, including several cell group leaders, work shifts. Less than a third own a car. There is great unity in the church, and a high level of commitment to growing in our knowledge of God. A number of people are excellent servants. We also have several that are highly creative. There is a considerable proportion for whom non-book forms of communication work best. Our regular corporate activities are Sunday morning meetings, cell groups, Alpha courses, and a monthly 'friendship and food' ministry to the local poor. We hold regular social events for bridge-building with not-yet-Christian friends. The pressures on time and energy of living in the inner city are a significant factor.

Links. We are part of a family of churches, some of which are quite large, which gives us access to some resources we lack. We also have links with a local group of churches that work together for prayer and training.

Leaders. There is currently one full time elder, myself. The lay leaders in the church are excellent, but live highly pressured lives. Finding more leaders is a constant challenge. I have not received formal theological training. I am probably better in small groups and one-to-one situations than larger, more formal settings. I have a wife and three children under the age of eight. I am involved in voluntary work, both for involvement in ministry to the poor, and as my main contact with not-yet-Christians. I am involved in various other projects such as occasional writing for a Christian magazine. All of these factors mean that my time is at a premium.

Developing a framework

Before developing ideas of which tools to use and how to apply them, it's helpful first of all to identify the ground we're trying to cover.

2 Corinthians 3:18 sets the agenda: the process of being changed into the likeness of Jesus. What does mean in practical terms? There's no right or wrong answer here, but it may be useful to unpack it into three main strands:

Being – developing the character of Jesus

Doing – behaving as Jesus did

Understanding – growing in wisdom

These can be sub-divided, as shown below, to provide a skeleton framework.

Being

1. Attitudes, attributes and qualities

The New Testament places a great deal of weight on character development. Whatever strategy we have will need to tackle this difficult area. Character qualities that are given high priority include for example:

- Love
- Perseverance
- Fruit of the Spirit
- Commitment
- Humility
- Obedience
- A serving heart
- Submission

2. Values

The Kingdom of God operates to a value system that is radically different from that of the world. Kingdom values are pervasive, they touch every aspect of our lives: there's no artificial spiritual/secular divide. To be like Jesus we need to recognise that there's no room for accommodating or trying to blend that which is irreconcilable: we need to be prepared to challenge our culture's values, and establish godly principles in areas such as:

- Money
- Time
- Leisure and comfort
- Priorities
- Health
- Power
- The home
- Sex
- Truth and honesty
- Work
- Unemployment
- Individualism
- Family

3. Breaking free

A central aspect of discipleship is becoming more like Jesus by 'putting off our old nature and putting on the new' (Eph 4:22–24). This involves understanding both what the old and new natures look like and practical ways of living by the Spirit. We may need to break free from:

- Jealousy
- Idolatry
- Desire for power
- Bitterness
- Independence
- Rage
- Gossip and slander
- Self-centredness
- Thirst for recognition
- Dishonesty

Doing

1. Life skills

The development of essential skills such as:

- How to hear God
- How to handle temptation
- How to pray
- How to make decisions
- How to study the Bible
- How to discern good and evil

- How to handle our emotions   • How to witness
  and thoughts

2. Serving: building others up

Disciples are called to be people who act on the Word, not merely hearers. Serving one another, and serving those in need in the world are central to our calling. A key aspect of helping people become like Jesus is releasing them into their purposes in God. This will include:

- Identifying a disciple's character, gifts, abilities, and experiences[1]
- Developing a servant heart
- Teaching how to work in a team, and under authority
- Deploying appropriately, with authority, responsibility and accountability

3. Godly living

Our society is rapidly losing touch with even the basics of Christian values of morality, and lifestyle. We simply can't afford to make any assumptions about what people understand. Our strategy will need to cover areas of everyday living that previous generations could take for granted. But changes in these areas of practical daily life are often the most visible to those around us and make us particularly contagious. Again, the scope is large; here for example are some subjects we might want to include:

- Honesty
- Keeping a marriage healthy
- Food
- Getting out of bad habits

- Making and keeping friends
- What we say
- Handling pressure

- Good sex
- How to raise kids
- How to handle money
- Dealing with negative thinking
- Self control: road rage
- Dealing with hard times
- Handling conflict

Understanding

I've left this section until last, partly as a challenge to the fact that in our church culture this so often takes precedence. In seeking to redress the balance though, it's vital that we don't under-emphasise this crucial area.

1. Doctrine

I think it's fairly obvious that all Christians need a clear, sound understanding of doctrines such as:

- God
- Holy Spirit
- Creation
- Sanctification
- Death
- New heaven and new earth
- Prayer
- Kingdom of God
- The Gospel
- Jesus
- Revelation
- Salvation
- Good and Evil
- New birth
- Church
- Second coming
- Spiritual warfare
- Disciple-making

2. Heart knowledge

The Bible often refers to the thoughts of our hearts. I think we need to recognise that it's one thing to 'know' a truth in our minds, another thing to know it in our hearts such that we live by it. It's important not to neglect this heart knowledge. To be radical disciples we need to know, deep inside ourselves:

- God's father heart towards us
- Assurance of salvation
- Hope
- Our love of Him
- Faith
- Our identity

3. Apologetics

The Bible calls us to be able to give an account of our faith. I think that this must include having something to say about the issues that not-yet-Christians identify as hurdles to their own response to God. More than this, I think that I need to encourage the church to see every aspect of life from a worldview that is God-centred. It's when we've seen the world from God's point of view can we begin to speak into it, challenge it and change it. We're not to live in a spiritual closet. We're in the world changing business. This is a potentially enormous field, and may take us into some unusual areas, because the world has some interesting obsessions. Some of the areas that we could look at include:

- Suffering
- Abortion
- The lottery
- Third World debt
- Scientific advances such as cloning
- Other religions
- Aliens
- Aids
- The paranormal

4. Church vision

Finally, I believe that the process of becoming like Jesus is rooted in the local church. My strategy will include ways of helping people have a clear focus on our purposes, vision, values, and practices as a local church[2].

Covering the ground

Understanding

Doctrine

We'll use the **sermon** as our main tool to teach doctrine. An important element of the strategy will be to continue to bring regular teaching to the church from **guest speakers**, especially those who are gifted teachers. This brings variety, and provides a safeguard given my lack of theological training.

Our core beliefs are set out in a **booklet**, given to all newcomers.

Doctrinal discussions will sometimes arise in **cell group** meetings. This is to be encouraged, as we want everyone to be confident and experienced at thinking biblically, although leaders will need to guard against the pooling of ignorance or being side-tracked into obscure areas.

Our family of churches runs **study breaks at the King's Bible College,** and I plan to attend some, both to strengthen my own understanding and to learn from seeing the teaching gift in operation.

The **'Workshop'**[3] course, is a valuable resource. Two of the congregation are currently on the course, and I may encourage another two to go next year.

Heart knowledge

Cell groups seem to be effective for tackling these areas. Knowing the fatherhood of God is a key subject to tackle this year. Sometimes **conferences** can be helpful, and we'll continue to encourage people to take advantage of them, although cost and time are problems. Often it's some form of experience or **encounter with God** that brings about a breakthrough, but this is difficult to plan!

Apologetics

I think these are best dealt with when issues arise. This will probably happen in one-to-one conversation or perhaps in the cell group context when people are discussing conversations they have had with not-yet-Christians. Some issues are raised in the **Alpha** courses. Our recent **men's night out** concluded with discussion long into the night, partly on these issues and would be well worth repeating.

Purpose, vision, values of the Church

In his book *The Purpose Driven Church*[4], Rick Warren recommends re-stating the church's vision every 26 days! And in as many different forms as possible. We'll probably primarily use the Sunday morning **sermon** when the whole congregation is gathered. The basics of the vision are stated on the **notice board** on the way in. We could use **OHP slides** and put them on the screen every week before and after the meeting. The **newcomers'**

booklet covers this ground. Every opportunity should be taken to reinforce the message in leaders' meetings.

Being

Attitudes, attributes, qualities

The Bible seems to indicate that growth in these areas often arises from godly responses to the trials of life. I think that this is a long term process, and very individual. It's hard to see how it can be programmed. I think the best contribution I can make is regular teaching on how **the mechanics** work, to encourage people to change their perspective on the **trials** they encounter. I can give regular examples when I'm teaching from the Bible and my own experiences.

Some of the attitudes can be **caught from others**. I can encourage people to see the areas where they are weaker and encourage them to rub shoulders with people they feel are further ahead. I need to assess my own standing in these areas so that through modelling, mentoring and personal pastoring I'm passing on life, not disease.

Values

I enjoy teaching on these issues in sermons, but we've also been covering them successfully in our cell groups. There's probably a case for developing a more planned approach as to what we cover in the 'Word' section of our cell meetings.

Breaking free

Again this is probably well suited to **cell groups**, and also to one-to-one **pastoral ministry** as issues arise.

Doing

Spiritual skills

We'll probably try to instil these in a variety of ways. **Modelling** from leaders is important. Applying these skills in **cell groups** is helpful. Recommending **books** can be effective, especially where we follow up to see how people have responded. Spiritual skills are also well communicated in workshop format in the course of a weekend **retreat**. I think we should aim to run two retreats a year: late spring and early autumn.

Serving

A good proportion of the congregation is actively serving in some capacity, although we are always struggling to find people willing to undertake the menial tasks. One difficulty is that in a church as small as ours the range of ministries and activities is relatively narrow. We may be able to take more advantage of the **wider family** of churches to which we belong. Some of them are large enough to have a number of specialised ministries. It may be possible to attach some of our folk to these projects.

Godly everyday living

These areas are well covered in **cell groups** through a combination of establishing Biblical principles, discussing how to apply them, inviting the Holy Spirit to empower, and then being accountable at the next meeting for applying what has been learned.

Using the tools

Sermons

For the 52 weeks in a year, my programme will be on these lines:

Renewing the vision	8 sessions
Guest speakers	10 sessions
Doctrine: thematic	10 sessions
Exegetical preaching	8 sessions
God's values	6 sessions
The Gospel	4 sessions
Unallocated	6 sessions

I'll need to flesh this out and decide specifically what to cover this year.

I plan to work on making my sermon style more **non-book**, especially by the use of stories, illustrations etc. I will look for opportunities to involve the congregation in learning experiences, while avoiding gimmicks.

Cell groups

These will continue as an integral part of the discipling process. The main task is to put together a programme to make sure that the 'Word' section in particular provides a balanced diet with clear objectives. Leadership training remains a high priority to make sure that the cell vision, especially the evangelistic thrust, remains in clear focus. We need to be training new leaders in anticipation of multiplying.

One-to-one

This is a major area that needs developing further, but I'm very conscious of the pressure of time. I think that too often my one-to-one work has been reactive, i.e. in response to people wanting help with a problem. I need to make sure I give quality input to those who are growing well. I need to train others in how to do this type of discipling. I am very engaged with the idea of **visits to the workplace**, perhaps for lunch, and praying about whatever issues people are facing there.

Retreats

We'll arrange weekend retreats for small groups twice a year, using my parents' home in order to minimise cost. These will be especially directed towards developing spiritual disciplines, and giving opportunity for times of withdrawal.

Looking at the different 'dimensions' of discipleship

By and large our discipling process has a reasonable balance of **knowledge, discovery** and **action.** Regular 'hands-on' prayer, especially in cell groups gives good opportunities for

encountering God and receiving fresh filling of His Holy Spirit's **power**. It may be possible to arrange for people in the congregation to go overseas with teams from other churches in our family, to **experience** God's work in the Third World. Time and money are, on the face of it, a limitation and we may need to pray about this. Sometimes visiting speakers or teams are occasions when breakthroughs take place. I'm afraid I don't like **confrontation**, but I need to ask God to help me see where it is necessary, and to do it with loving boldness. As for **crises**, I think that when they arise, I need to encourage the church to respond with faith, seeing them as an opportunity to grow and mature.

Patterns of growth

Location. I would like to make more regular use of visiting the workplace. As usual the constraints of time imply that my ambitions should be modest for the time being.

Accountability. Cell groups place a healthy emphasis on accountability for what we are learning, with regular 'homework' and opportunity for feedback. Cell leaders have a clear job description to which I hold them accountable. I need to make sure I continue to do this!

Patterns of growth and pacing. This is primarily a matter of awareness, so that leaders in particular have reasonable expectations.

Questions and answers. When preparing sermons, I will endeavour to identify those areas which might best be tackled by posing questions, rather than by giving answers.

Non-book culture. I will review my sermon style. Cell groups have quite a strong non-book approach. I will encourage those who have access to the Internet to tap into the vast resources of Christian material that are available.

Concluding thoughts

This strategy contains a number of new initiatives. Given the scarcity of leaders in the church, it may not be possible to implement more than a few at a time, so prioritising may be necessary. Since some of the approaches are experimental, it will be necessary to review the results honestly and thoroughly.

SUMMARY

Drawing up a strategy for making contagious Christians is a healthy discipline, helping us take the step from idea to application. Every church is unique: the plans for making dangerous, contagious Christians in a congregation which is multi-cultural, urban and poor will be significantly different to a church that is homogeneous, middle-class and suburban. We have to stay flexible, and to keep asking the same questions: *What gets the job done best? What is most effective?*

Part III

UNCAGED

Chapter 10

'... AND FORCEFUL MEN ...'

The salt pot may be full. The lamp may be brim full of oil. But the salt must be shaken, and the lamp lit in order to be effective. Ultimately we're only truly contagious if the fullness of life within us overflows; touches the world. But this can only happen if we break free of the values, attitudes and mindsets that hold us in their grip, stifling our potential. In these last three chapters, let's do some cutting free. . . .

An evening out

Jesus and the disciples were tired. It had been quite a day. Jesus had taught and ministered to a large crowd, so large in fact that he'd had to preach from a boat on the lake. He'd given them as much as they could handle. In between telling parables to the crowds, he'd sat down with the disciples and explained everything to them. The evening had come, the crowd dispersed. Jesus had told the disciples they would cross over the lake. The disciples had been looking for some rest, and Jesus himself had fallen asleep. Suddenly, out of nowhere, a terrifying storm had blown up. The disciples, even the seasoned fishermen, had been scared witless, expecting to drown. Jesus had been awesome, standing up there, rebuking the wind, commanding the waves to be still: and they were! And now finally, they were approaching the other shore, completely exhausted, soaking wet, ready for some food and sleep.

But now as they approach the shore in the gathering gloom, the disciples realise that of all places, they're coming in to land near the burial areas. Everyone knows that evil spirits live in places like this, and night is when they emerge, when they're most powerful. The disciples are distinctly uneasy, peering through the gloom, as Jesus steps out of the boat. Suddenly, there's a terrifying unearthly scream, and something comes charging towards them out of the gathering darkness, yelling like the devil himself, flailing metal chains. A complete maniac, his clothes in rags, his body cut and bleeding, his face contorted with rage and pain, bearing down on them, closer, closer . . .

(From Mark 4 and 5, retold in my own words.)

Mark 5, where the story continues, makes no further mention of the disciples. My suspicion is that they set a new record for paddling a fishing boat across the Sea of Galilee! But Jesus didn't flinch an inch. Even at the end of an exhausting day, He had nerves of steel. He certainly had 'bottle'. In fact, if we can just take our blinkers off, set aside our preconceptions for a moment, we find that the Jesus we read about in the Gospels was a force to be reckoned with.

The Jesus of the Gospels

Jesus was physically strong. Let's face it, when He cleared the temple, it's unlikely that the market stalls holders sat passively by and watched Him dump their stuff all over the ground; we're looking at a major fracas here. Jesus not only over-turned the tables but drove everyone out of the temple area with a whip. When the crowd sought to push Him off a cliff, He muscled his way through them and went on his way. He could probably have torn a phone book in half: after all He'd spent his life since childhood in a carpenter's workshop in an age before power tools. Anybody who could walk after the beating he received before His crucifixion must have been very tough.

Jesus didn't just overturn tables, he overturned pretty well every convention of his age. He gave one-to-one teaching to women; he spoke with Samaritans; he fraternised with the Romans; he touched the untouchable; he befriended prostitutes and fraudsters; he welcomed the rejected; he healed on the Sabbath.

Jesus knew how to upset people. He trashed the temple market; he sent someone's entire pig business plunging into the lake in a time before they had insurance for that kind of thing. He upset his family; He put his disciples on the spot; He humiliated his opponents; He made clever people look foolish. He humbled the arrogant; left religious leaders with egg on their faces, gave a young ruler a hard time, and even threw down a tough challenge to someone who was recently bereaved. You'd have to say that he was a hard hitter.

Jesus also amazed people, He delighted them. He stretched them, challenged them, changed them, healed them, set them free, and made them laugh. He reached rich and poor, children and the elderly; men and women, bondsman and free, Jew and Gentile, peasants and professionals, believers and sceptics, artisans and intellectuals. He turned the world upside down, he made the slave free and the freeman a slave; He called the humble great and the great nothing; He comforted the afflicted and afflicted the comfortable. He took on Satan himself and comprehensively defeated him. He opened the door to unity with God, to victory over death, and life to the full.

Jesus was often up all night, usually in demand all day; He was criticised, gossiped about, misunderstood. People tried to trap Him, people tried to manipulate Him, people tried to force him into their mould. Many people deserted Him, even his disciples often didn't understand Him and one of them betrayed Him. In all of this, Jesus was never grumpy or irritable; He was never proud or selfish; He was never cynical or despairing; and He never sought revenge. He never lost his nerve, He never lost His focus, He never took short cuts; He never made mistakes and He never lost His self-control. In fact He lived through all of this without once committing a single sin. Awesome.

How, from this, did we end up with the Jesus portrayed in so many of our churches: 'Mr Nice Guy'?

Whereas Mary wrapped Jesus in swaddling bands, we seem to have wrapped Him in layers of politeness and middle-class behaviour, made Him comfortable to us. We've tried to massage away that which we felt to be embarrassing or hard to explain or which we felt might be unattractive to our friends. But it hasn't worked. All we've succeeded in doing is portraying Jesus in ways that seem completely irrelevant to people's lives, and impotent to change them. Incredibly, we have managed to make the most radical and electrifying man who ever walked the earth boring to many people. The early church, for all it's problems and weaknesses was lean, agile and vigorous; we seem to have become altogether too well padded. Perhaps this is one of the reasons we still haven't seen a real breakthrough in drawing significant numbers to our churches yet. I suspect that we have an exciting and (probably hair-raising) journey of rediscovery ahead of us, stepping out of our church conditioning and learning to see the Jesus of the Bible.

Kingdom manhood

The debate about women in leadership, and the predominance of men in positions of authority in churches has somewhat obscured the fact that the church in the UK has found it particularly difficult to attract men, especially outside the middle classes. But Jesus had absolutely no trouble at all: He preached to 5,000 men on one occasion, and had a team of men, from a variety of backgrounds who had left everything to follow Him.

Clearly the Gospel is not inherently unattractive to men, and the success of the 'Promise Keepers'[1] in the USA endorses this. This suggests that we should take a hard look instead at the way we have communicated the message, and the way that we have run 'church'. The following are necessarily generalisations, but points that I think we should consider.

- Men in general like to be active; but by and large we've made church life passive and talk orientated. It's good that we value prayer in our churches. But prayers are never effective when they're being used as a substitute for action. If we study the Bible carefully we may be shocked to find that we're doing what we should be praying about and praying when we should be doing. For example there are virtually no references at all to praying our not-yet-Christian friends into the Kingdom. Rather it's up to us to 'go' and 'tell' them, as we were instructed. Evangelistic prayer in the Bible is always directed to the *Christians*, for boldness, power and opportunity.
- Men respect strength and vigour; but we've emphasised Jesus' meekness and humility. It's true that Jesus was meek: but it was the meekness of awesome capability in absolute control. It's true that Jesus was humble, but we so often use the word 'humble' as a spiritual disguise for lack of confidence, low self-esteem and opting out of responsibility. Authentic humility is not about despising ourselves: on the contrary, it's about seeing things as they truly are; it's recognising our value, seen in the context of the infinite greatness of God.
- Men need a clear sense of identity, but we have talked about 'death to self'. It's true that we are to die to self, but this is not about becoming non-persons. Quite the opposite: the Scriptures are calling us to die to selfishness, to put off the selfish nature, so that we can become fully who we are meant to be. And the Bible says a great deal about who we are: new creations, sons of the King, royal priests, ambassadors of

Christ, salt of the earth, light of the world, a city on a hill, heirs of God, more than conquerors, God's fellow workers, a sacred temple, citizens of heaven, a chosen people, a holy nation, a Kingdom for God.

- Men like to participate, to make a difference, rather than to be spectators, yet we've made Christianity disengaged from most parts of life, caged up in meetings, in set times of the day, confined to 'spiritual' matters. But the true Gospel of the Kingdom engages every aspect of life; it is extensive, invasive, pervasive and offensive.

- Men like to fight, but we've given them fund-raising and the church accounts. The Gospel calls us to engage in spiritual warfare; to combat the enemy's attacks in our own lives; to fight for truth and justice; to defend the weak and powerless; to wrestle with the false and destructive values prevailing in our society; and to take a stand for honesty and integrity in a corrupt culture. Ruthlessness is probably the most undervalued Christian virtue. The Bible says that God is a warrior (Ex 15:3). We tend to think of this in the context of a fallen world full of evil and warfare against Satan. But what about in the new heaven and new earth, when Satan has been defeated, sin wiped out, and death swallowed up in life? God will *still* be a warrior because He is unchanging. Being a warrior is not simply God's response to a situation, it is part of His nature. Although we abhor the war we see in this world, there is something for us to discover in the heart of a warrior that is godly. God has given us forward facing eyes: we have the face of a predator.

- Men like a vision, a goal, something to work for. We've offered a view of heaven where we sing songs for eternity. But the Bible talks of our destiny to rule nations, to have Satan crushed beneath our feet. It speaks of a new heaven and a new earth where we will fulfil our destiny to reign with God, to work, to grow, to adventure for all eternity, freed from all the limitations and frustrations of this fallen world.

In the end we need to learn that we don't have to apologise for Jesus. We don't need to package Him, to market Him, to act as His spin-doctors. If our self-esteem is based on feeling successful through building up our church's attendance, then yes, there is always the temptation to compromise the truth in some way to entice people into our churches. Ultimately it doesn't work because people are designed to want the truth, to be dissatisfied with anything less. We're building with hay and straw. When our self-esteem is based on our true identity as God's children, it becomes easier to understand that it's His church; He will build it, and He will build it the way He chooses.

SUMMARY

There's an exciting adventure of rediscovery ahead of us if we're willing to break out of our cosy preconceptions and meet the Jesus of the Bible. Similarly, if we have a fresh encounter with the Gospel of the Scriptures, we will be invigorated, and also find that we have a message that is much more attractive to men.

Jesus' work is to prepare his bride, and to see the Kingdom of God established over all. Wonderfully He's invited us to join Him, to take part in what He's doing. As we work with Him, we are being transformed into His likeness, becoming what He longs for us to be: dangerous disciples.

Chapter 11

BREAKING OUT

You can keep a herd of cattle contained by installing cattle grids. But once the cattle are familiar with them, you can 'install' new ones simply by painting them on the road. Even new cows joining the herd will not cross them. Our mindsets too can imprison us and prevent our contagious life reaching the world. It is time to cross the line. It is time to switch from the defensive to the offensive.

Fear of pollution

Evangelicalism has a strong current of 'holiness' teaching. The call to be holy is entirely biblical, but the key questions it raises are 'What does it mean?' and 'How do we do it?' Many Christians see the world as fundamentally an evil and dangerous place, with the capability to corrupt and pollute. With this mindset the call to holiness can easily become a strategy of withdrawal, and before long we become preoccupied with endless debates on what is and isn't appropriate activity for Christians; what books, films, TV shows, and music should be avoided. We're living fearfully, on the defensive. Before we know it we've adopted a ghetto mentality, lobbing the occasional truth grenade over the wall and ducking for cover.

This has some very serious implications:

Disconnected. Firstly, the ghetto mentality cuts us off from so much of the activities of those around us, making it much harder to be salt and light to them. We make it harder for ourselves both to understand the issues our not-yet-Christian friends are facing, and to find common ground for communicating life to them. Although the Fall has had a tremendously damaging effect, humanity nevertheless bears the mark of the image of God, however marred. We know that creation is still capable of declaring the glory of God; we know that human governmental authorities are to be respected and honoured because God is still willing to work through them, flawed though they evidently are. The New Testament teaches that while we are not to be of the world, we are nevertheless to be in it. Paul tells the Corinthians to dissociate themselves from deceptive and immoral brothers, but specifically emphasises that He doesn't mean them to become separate from unbelievers. Jesus had no problem in providing alcohol for a wedding, attending a party thrown by a tax collector and receiving the attentions of a known prostitute, all actions which shocked the religious leaders of His day.

In contrast we tend to withdraw from the areas where we feel uncertain or uncomfortable. In doing so we risk cutting our connections to not-yet-Christians around us, and effectively sending a signal that there are no-go zones for the Gospel, areas where we have nothing to say. We need to be willing to see the films, watch the TV shows, read the newspapers that set and define the world's agenda in order to engage it effectively with the Gospel. When you know your soil type, you know how best to sow your seed. Let me give an extreme example: we may talk in our churches about the 'truth', but in reality a large proportion of the population thinks that the 'truth is out there' (the X-files perspective) and the possibility of alien life forms is a source of huge fascination. How many of our church members can engage in a discussion about aliens, and through it present a Kingdom perspective?

Perhaps we're concerned that people will criticise. Should we as Christians be seen in such places or talk about such things? But maybe our reputation is a luxury we can't afford if it means denying the lost access to life. Jesus was quite willing to have His reputation rest on the opinion of His Father, not the comments of men. Perhaps we fear that somehow we will be drawn into sinful activity, or be exposed to things that are depraved and uncomfortable. Clearly we need to be wise, to be aware of our weaknesses and limitations. Equally though we should look to train ourselves in discernment, in overcoming temptation, and become more disciplined in asking God to cleanse our hearts and minds from the slime we encounter living in a fallen world. I think we're called to rise to the challenge, not to run from it.

Skewed message. Secondly, a ghetto mentality skews our message. Our Gospel is 'life to the full', but most not-yet-Christians think that it's a long list of things they're not allowed to do. The incarnation, crucifixion, resurrection and Pentecost together signalled D-Day, the invasion of enemy territory by the Kingdom of God, the beginning of a conquering advance culminating in total victory. As Jesus put it: 'From the days of John the Baptist until now, the kingdom of heaven has been forcefully advancing, and forceful men lay hold of it' (Matt 11:12). Although we're part of the D-Day army, we often behave as though we're calling people to be part of the Dunkirk remnant. Instead of inviting them to share in the victory, we offer fellowship in the grim struggle to survive and remain pure in a dirty world. Instead of inviting people to join an advancing Kingdom that will transform the world for good, we ask them to help us rescue a few souls near enough for us to reach. But the Scriptures offer more than mere survival in life:

'. . . how much more will those who receive God's abundant provision of grace and of the gift of righteousness **reign in life** through the one man, Jesus Christ' (Rom 5:17).

Cut off. Thirdly, a ghetto mentality cuts us off from so much revelation from God. Shocking though it may seem, God doesn't seem to feel obliged to communicate exclusively to Christians or only through recognised 'Christian' channels. In fact He seems quite prepared to speak through whatever means He sees fit. In the Scriptures He reveals Himself to and through people who don't know or acknowledge Him, whether it be dreams to Pharaoh, visions to Persian emperors, or insights to Greek poets. I see no reason to doubt that in our own times God can and does communicate through television, films, and advertising posters. But the ghetto mentality drives us towards labelling some activities as spiritual and others not, and we begin to live in 'spiritual' enclaves disconnected from much of our 'ordinary' life and cut off from God's revelation therein. It's a recipe for stunted growth.

Indwelling. Fourthly, and perhaps most serious of all, the ghetto mentality demeans the power of what God has done within us. It undervalues the scale of what it means to be born again, to have a new nature, to be the dwelling place of the living God. It assumes that the world's power to corrupt us is greater than our power in Jesus to change the world. It may seem shocking to say these things, and most of us would vigorously deny that this has any part in our theology, but sometimes we betray ourselves in our behaviour. We see it, for example, in the tendency for Christians starting a family to move out of the urban areas, rather than face raising children there.

The education ghetto

At the risk of being controversial, I think we should take a hard look at the growing number Christian schools. From small beginnings, there are now scores of them across the country, with more opening up all the time. The basic philosophy behind this is that state schools are now such godless places, promoting unhealthy values, and exposing our children to other religions. Therefore, the argument goes, we cannot allow our children to go there. But isn't this an example of ghetto mentality? Surely the people of God are meant to go to the godless places to bring life and light to people and institutions lost in darkness. Withdrawing our involvement both in terms of pupils and parental input to the schools is surely the last thing we should be doing. It's difficult to see how we can be claiming to prepare our children to be witnesses when we've placed them in an environment where there are few or none to witness to. It's difficult to see how we are equipping them to bring the Gospel to a needy world when we've closeted them away in another world entirely. It's equally difficult to feel that we can communicate the power of the Gospel to them when by our actions we've sent a signal that we're afraid of the world, scared that its power to corrupt is greater than God's power to transform and heal. It seems to me to be a short step, in concept at least, from this mentality to saying that Christians should only go to Christian universities, and work for Christian firms, use Christian banks and shops.

I accept the point that many Christian schools take children from not-yet-Christian families. Clearly these will be families with the financial means to pay for private education. This takes us back to a point I expressed at the start of this book: we're unlikely to break out of our middle class bridgehead if so many of our resources are invested in reinforcing it. We have to be willing to be radical, to redirect those resources, if we're serious about striking more deeply into fresh territory.

My heart cry is that we go a different route: that we increase our involvement in state schools rather than withdraw from them. I propose that we do more to encourage parents on to governing bodies of schools; that we should increase the number of teams going into schools to run assemblies and help with classes. I believe there's a lot more scope for supporting Christian teachers working in state schools. There's a great deal that we can learn about equipping parents, helping them to grasp their role as the primary educators of their children in the ways of God, and to develop the know-how to support their children in the challenges they face in the classroom. It's a case of developing a style of Christianity that's practical, confident, and robust. But all this can only begin when we mentally escape the ghetto.

'If in doubt . . .'

This fear of pollution has the effect of determining our defaults, that is to say, our basic reactions to the new or unfamiliar. By and large our defaults are set to 'if in doubt, throw it out'. There's a strong tendency to assume that everything is suspect unless we can prove otherwise. In fact we have a raft of vocabulary to express the point, ranging from 'unsound' to 'off the wall' depending on one's place in the Christian spectrum. It's always interesting to see Christians' reactions when I talk to them about learning from the Catholic contemplative tradition, or learning from the Orthodox Church about the use of art in worship. Often the initial reaction, almost a reflex, is one of suspicion, doubt and concern. The response to mention of activities such as Tai Chi or acupuncture is usually closer to horror, even when the listener knows next to nothing about the subject. A strong suspicion of alien cultures, (especially those of the East) is deeply embedded in our default system. But the question is this: are these the appropriate default settings?

The Apostle Paul seems to operate rather differently. In his teaching in Romans 14 and 1 Corinthians 10 he exhorts the early Christians not to be bound by rules and fears about food. The basic principle is to assume that everything is suitable for eating without question, with two exceptions: if it would damage one's own conscience, or present a stumbling block to others. Even where we graciously give way for the sake of our brother's conscience, we are not to allow what we consider good to be spoken of as evil (Rom 14:16). Elsewhere Paul exhorts Christians not to be bound by anxieties about keeping special days and festivals. In 1 Corinthians 6 Paul states his basic position, that 'everything is permissible, but not everything is beneficial'. He repeats this same phrase in chapter 10, adding by way of explanation 'The earth is the Lord's and everything in it'.

Paul's basic position is to stand in the place of confidence and freedom, unless there are special circumstances to consider. His starting point is 'Everything God created is good, and nothing is to be rejected if it is received with thanksgiving' (1 Tim 4:4). This is not to say that he advocates an 'anything goes' policy: clearly he doesn't. He's careful to say that not everything is beneficial, that there are circumstances where we temper our freedom for the sake of another. His default is based on a supreme confidence in the greatness of God, a God who 'richly provides us with everything for our enjoyment' (1 Tim 6:17), a God who 'did not give us a spirit of timidity, but a spirit of power, love and self-discipline' (2 Tim 1:7).

We can easily become afraid of making mistakes or of being led into error and so we protect ourselves, avoiding anything we consider risky. Our lives quickly become narrow. But the New Testament calls us to a different way of living, trusting in God as our Protector. We have a God who is greater than our mistakes; we have the indwelling of the Holy Spirit whose revelation of truth is our best defence against error; we have a new nature which bears the fruit of self-control to guard us against rashness. Living this way, our lives become expansive and confident; we see life as an adventure and the world around us as an exciting place where we can learn about God in a huge variety of ways. Paul gave a simple instruction to the

Thessalonians: 'Test everything, hold fast to that which is good' (1 Thess 5:21). When we give ourselves permission to explore, my experience is that we understand new things precisely because we've seen them from a different perspective. If they're true we'll find them there in Scripture, under our noses after all, only needing a fresh eye to see them.

The choice is ours: do we refuse to eat fish because it has bones? And miss out on all the enjoyment and nourishment? Surely it's a better choice by far to delight in eating fish, confident that we will spit out the bones when we find them.

It's time to reset our defaults.

Breaking the walls of glass

Walls of glass may be transparent, indeed we may not even be aware of them. But they can cage us in nevertheless. It's scary when we begin to realise the extent of unspoken rules that govern our thoughts and actions, patterns of accepted behaviour to which we're expected to conform. It's noticeable that even after major change new walls discreetly emerge; our hard won freedom quickly becomes a new set of norms. For example, having broken free of some of the constraints of old style formal liturgy, it has proved very difficult not to simply substitute one of our own: it may be informal, but it can be just as restrictive. If we're not careful we simply swap an old formula for a new one. When we live by invisible rules we begin to exclude those who don't conform to them, the opposite of our calling to reach out to all those different from ourselves. When we live by invisible rules we unconsciously exclude ourselves from some experiences of God: it simply doesn't occur that God might work in such a way. God doesn't want us to live by formulas, behind these walls of glass; He wants us to break out into the glorious freedom we have in Him.

Let me give an example. In my own church recently, as we were singing songs of praise and worship, two people brought prophetic words which indicated that the Holy Spirit wanted to bring comfort and healing to certain people, including my wife, Charlotte. We decided to pray in small groups for those people. Before we did so, however, the Holy Spirit intervened and said that often as we pray we tend to focus on the problem and find our faith wilting in the face of it. As an alternative, we were to look instead to God, and to sing our prayers and praises, simply holding the person we were praying for up before Him. We were reminded of the Scripture which talks of 'singing and making music in our heart to God' (Eph 5:19), and of the references in the Old Testament to the army of the Israelites being led into battle by musicians and worshippers. Some people were slightly thrown, perhaps by self-consciousness about their singing voice, perhaps because this way of praying for someone was already challenging their idea of accepted behaviour. Nevertheless the prayer/singing began with a strong sense of the presence of God. But there was another surprise to come. Charlotte who had been standing in the midst of a group of people ministering to her, suddenly felt led by the Spirit to express her joy for God by leaping and dancing around the room. Her team of prayer-singers straggled after her like geese! We met the Lord power-fully, and we also experienced tremendous freedom, a sense of having broken through one of these glass walls. Why was this?

When we reflected, we understood that without realising it we had become trapped within glass walls about how ministry, or praying for people, should take place. Unconsciously we had adopted a set of pre-suppositions. These said that the person being prayed for should remain still, with eyes closed, looking down, perhaps with hands raised, open to receive from God. And that the people praying should gather around, perhaps placing their hands on the person, and that they should pray earnest prayers with intense expressions on their faces, looking as though they were laying spiritual eggs. These suppositions had no place when trying to sing while scrambling after the subject of the prayer as she pirouetted into the distance!

God has continued to show us other glass barriers. Indeed He's training us to see them more clearly, and to develop the habit of breaking them. They usually seem so obvious that it's hard to imagine how we didn't see them before. And when we do there is a sense of excitement from the prospect of finding what's on the other side, of exploring new territory. Recently, the Lord has been challenging us on the extent to which our worship has become front-led, with a predictable sound and format. He's been encouraging us to explore a wide range of different ways of worshipping Him, releasing that huge creative potential within each one of us made in His image. We're taking a few steps closer to what the Bible calls for: worshipping Him with every dimension of our humanity.

We're finding that as we break through some of these glass barriers, we develop a habit of questioning everything, challenging all our assumptions, exploring new areas, and always testing everything against the Bible. It's not so much that we're finding out what the Bible allows us to do, but rather we're discovering that there's so little that God has *not* allowed us to do. It's another change of defaults: instead of assuming we need specific permission to try something, we assume that we can do anything unless God precludes it. As we develop this habit corporately, we're finding that it spills over into our family life and our personal walk with God. We find ourselves stepping forward into virgin territory, sniffing the air, seeing familiar landmarks from new perspectives, and, just for those first few steps, hearing the sound of broken glass crunching beneath our feet.

It's breakout time for the people of God.

SUMMARY

Christians are born free, and have everywhere put themselves in chains.

While inner transformation is central to our becoming contagious Christians, it's vital too that we break through certain attitudes and values that can act like glass barriers: hard to see, but nevertheless constraining us. A defensive worldview and our fear of being polluted have pushed us into a ghetto mentality. We find it hard to fulfil our calling to be salt and light, and we miss many of God's expressions of Himself, and the joy that comes from such discoveries. We run the risk of barricading our spirituality into an enclave cut off from much of 'normal' life. We run the risk of underrating the power of God working within us.

We default towards rejecting the unfamiliar. This can make our lives narrow and limited. We need instead to choose biblical confidence and freedom, to be willing to test everything, holding on to that which is good, rejecting that which isn't. It's time to reset our defaults.

We can be trapped in our presuppositions and assumptions about how to behave in our corporate activities and in our individual lives. We need to be willing to break these glass walls. Jesus said his mission was to 'release the captives'; I think he'd like to start with Christians.

The New Testament constantly reminds us of the awesome truth that God indwells his people, and that 'greater is He that is in us is than he that is in the world' (1 John 4:4). In short, Followers of the Way are called to be an overcoming people, confident, on the offensive. We are to be invasive and pervasive, plundering the enemy's kingdom, pulling down his strongholds, changing everything and everyone we touch by exposing it to the love and truth of God. Legend talks of a King Midas, at whose touch everything turned to gold. In a sense, we are designed to be Midas people.

Chapter 12

CONTAGIOUS EVANGELISM

In the 19th Century, settlers from squalid overcrowded British cities emigrated to the vast spaciousness of Australia. But many of them built tiny houses in back-to-back terraces, without even a garden. Old habits die hard. Our society is changing so rapidly that in the same way, we, as Christians, stand blinking at the edge of new territory. What will we build?

There's really no option but to re-evaluate, and ruthlessly. Throughout this book I've argued the need to change our perspective on what it is to be a Christian. The challenge is to be so full of life as to overflow, become contagious.

Yet even then, retaining obsolete mindsets for evangelism will act as a bottleneck, it will blunt our impact. It's time to jettison the baggage. We need to think in fresh ways about the way we communicate the Gospel message itself: this is explored in the Appendix. But more than that, we need a radical overhaul of our models of evangelism. Painful perhaps, but a vital step closer to what we all long to see in our nation: an epidemic of Life.

Challenging our models of evangelism[1]

Evangelists or witnesses?

The sad truth is that in most churches evangelism is the domain of a handful of dedicated 'evangelists'. They provide the motive energy for evangelistic activities, while the rest of the church tends to opt out or provide only fringe support. This just will not suffice any longer. Our starting point must be to place the responsibility for evangelism firmly where it belongs: with every Christian. This is a practical imperative: there are simply not enough 'evangelists' in our churches to have the impact we need on society. And it's a biblical necessity: the word we translate 'evangelist' is used only three times in the New Testament; the word for 'witness' is used almost seventy times. Equipping and releasing every Christian as a witness has to be priority. Evangelism was never intended to be the ministry of the specialist, but the responsibility of a contagious people.

Relationships first!

Currently many evangelistic strategies place events, of varying kinds, at the start of the process. Establishing relationships follows later, when someone has made a commitment and been added to the church. But we need to turn this on its head. In a post-modern society, where absolutes of truth are denied, and where we can no longer assume even the most basic knowledge of Christian beliefs, evangelism works better when we recognise that *belonging* comes before *believing* and *relationships* before *response*. People are less interested than they used to be in 'Is it true?'; they're more interested in 'Does it work?'.

Coming or going?

Our models for evangelism are often based on the assumption that our goal is to draw people to the church, the invitation to *come*. We need to reverse this, to create a new expectation based on *Go!*. The onus is upon us to go and build relationships with not-yet-Christians, to go to their turf rather than expecting them to accommodate to us. This is a central tenet of Cell church thinking: that all Christians should give priority to developing a network of around three or four close unsaved friends. Whether a church works in cells or not, the principle remains valid: after all it was Jesus who said 'Go into all the world . . .'(Mark 16:15).

Of course, this is great in theory and much harder to achieve in practice. Church leaders need to be ruthless at cutting back on church activities and meetings to release time for relationship building. And it's no small task to break Christians out of their 'huddle' mentality. Currently, many Christians spend nearly all of their time with other Christians: it's safe, familiar, comfortable. Changing direction, giving priority to time with the not-yet-Christian requires a willingness to change lifestyle and routine, and good measures of courage and perseverance. We need to start equipping people in our churches with inter-personal skills, training them in the art of making friends.

Community before events

Much of our current evangelistic thinking looks to events as the platform for communicating the gospel. Posters and leaflets advertise to the public, and Christians are encouraged to 'bring a friend'. But in a post-modern society, where spirituality is increasingly regarded as a private rather than a public affair, this will be less and less relevant. We need to re-orientate. We'll be more effective when we think primarily in terms of including not-yet-Christians into our community, a network of Christian relationships where they will be welcomed, accepted, valued and loved. It's here where they can see the Gospel in action. They can try before they buy. It seems only reasonable: after all, we'll be asking them to sign their old life away.

This means that our Sunday morning meetings, relatively impersonal, and characterised by potentially alienating behaviour (in worship, for example), are the last place that we should invite our friends. The sense of community offered by small groups is likely to be far more attractive. Seeing the evangelistic potential of community in our homes and challenging the fixation we have with church buildings and meetings is a key shift of perception.

Extending the Kingdom

Although drawing not-yet-Christians into our community should be our aim, we also have to come to terms with the realities of modern urban life: namely that our lives are much less geographically defined. In cities people typically live in one area, work in another and socialise somewhere else again. For many Christians their primary evangelistic opportunity is not with their neighbours (who they may barely know) but with their colleagues at work with whom they spend many hours a day and share many of life's ups and downs. Yet many churches find that their whole evangelistic strategy is based on reaching into the local area in the vicinity of the church building. Not that this is wrong, simply that we need to add a dimension, to grasp the importance of equipping people to be effective witnesses in their main mission field: the workplace. We have to face the fact that successful evangelism here is unlikely to add numbers to our own church: the challenge is to lift our vision, to think in terms of extending the kingdom, rather than building our own church.

Crisis or process?

What is the goal of evangelism? Typically, the perceived aim is to provoke a 'crisis' moment of response, i.e. that people give their lives to the Lord when the Gospel is preached. A major problem now is that many people in a post-Christian society simply don't have enough background understanding to make their response to a twenty minute Gospel message very meaningful. Presenting the Gospel primarily in this way skews the emphasis of salvation towards an event rather than a process. And it puts the focus on what we're saved *from* rather than what we're saved *for*: a lifestyle of discipleship.

We have to come to terms with the fact that most people are almost completely ignorant of Christian beliefs – indeed their thinking is typically very confused by the bewildering array of belief systems prevalent in our society. Given this, evangelism needs to be redefined: it's not simply the business of winning converts: it's *everything* that helps someone take a step forward in their understanding of God and their relationship with Him. It's a process. Once we've grasped this we can break out of the crushing sense of failure that comes from crediting conversions as the sole measure of success. When we understand the enormous scope embraced in evangelism, it becomes far easier for Christians to feel that they can play a role. They no longer need feel impotent in evangelism because they lack the confidence to 'press for a decision'. When we define evangelism in this way it becomes a team activity. Fishing for men is a family business, with shared nets, not a loner with a rod and line.

Expound or explore?

The bottom line is that we're not simply looking for people to assent to a set of beliefs, to sign up for church attendance, or make a decision of the moment. We're looking to make disciples, people who know the Gospel, understand the cost and who have made a lifetime decision. Once we've taken hold of this, it's an easier step from the arrogance of 'telling someone the answers', the 'you're wrong, we're right' philosophy, to an approach that aims to help people to explore and engage with the Truth for themselves. This means we have to be willing to address the issues and questions they have, to meet with them where they are, rather than where we think they should be. This is not to suggest that we tailor the content of the Gospel so that it fits people comfortably. Rather, it's helping people understand the Gospel in such a way that their decision to follow Christ has depth, because they've seen and considered its implications for all the aspects of their lives that are important to them.

'I've started . . . so I'll finish'

Because we've been so locked into the idea of conversion as the goal of evangelism, it has for many become the high point of the Christian life too. Our theology of discipleship is vague and our strategy for growing to maturity haphazard. Our churches are full of Christians whose testimony is synonymous with their conversion story, who pine to recover their first love. Sadly, of our converts, all too many calcify into 'church-goers', or drift away. We need a radical response to this, placing a new emphasis on what we're saved for – transformation into the likeness of Jesus – and developing strategies to help people grow to maturity.

Visiblity

There's tremendous encouragement when a number of people respond at a public event and go forward at the altar call. Probably most of us have a dream of revival that envisions packed meeting halls, crowds falling to their knees in repentance. But is this the only form that revival can take? Is it an appropriate expectation in our present society? It's instructive to compare different experiences in the New Testament. In Acts 2 Peter preaches to the Jewish crowd in Jerusalem. They already have a good measure of understanding about God, and Peter preaches primarily from the Hebrew scriptures. There is a mass response of repentance and three thousand are saved that day. By contrast, in Acts 17, Paul's missionary journey to the Greek cities has a very different flavour. In Athens he reasons and debates, he starts his preaching by a reference to one of their gods and quotes one of their poets. Only a few respond, and many want to hear more. In Corinth he reasons and persuades, and stays for a full year and a half teaching. No mass conversions here, and yet we know that in the course of a few years there are large flourishing churches in these cities and throughout the area. Our own present-day society in the UK is probably a much closer match to Paul's audience than Peter's. Maybe we need to adjust our mental image: perhaps revivals can be huge without necessarily being high profile. Does our desire for a high visibility revival reveal something about our own motives?

Strategy

So much of our energies in evangelism centre on events and activities, designed to reap a harvest of new birth. But for many churches, the serious deficiencies in sowing and watering preceding this, severely limits the scale of the crop. Equally, in emphasising new principles of relationship building, process and exploration as central to evangelism, it's critical that we don't founder in a sea of vague good intentions that have no cutting edge. The harvest must be gathered, or it spoils. Laurence Singlehurst, in his brilliant book *Sowing, Reaping, Keeping*[2], hits the nail on the head: we need to plan, to have a strategy that encompasses sowing, watering, reaping and keeping. Maintaining the balance is how we stay productive. A strategy of *sowing* through developing networks of relationships, *reaping* through Alpha and Y courses and *keeping* by building people into cell groups, is already proving highly effective for some churches.

Re-evaluating our mindsets, and challenging our models is difficult, even painful. What if we make mistakes? Well, let's face it: for most churches, if we look closely at our current performance, do we really have that much to lose?

SUMMARY

We live in a world where people live lives of 'quiet desperation'.[3] It's a world that's crying out for contagious Christians who are full of life. We need to nurture that life within, to find ways of releasing it to maximum effect, and removing any bottlenecks that get in the way. This challenges us to rethink our preconceptions and models of evangelism. It's truly time to turn the Church inside out.

EPILOGUE

- Jesus had confidence
- Jesus was kind and compassionate but never a wimp
- Jesus was strong, but never abused his strength
- Jesus was never envious
- Jesus wasn't afraid to challenge wrong, and face opposition
- Jesus didn't feel insecure or inadequate
- Jesus was free of ambition and the drive for success
- Jesus wasn't hardened by his experiences
- Jesus was never sarcastic, never indulged in cynicism, never gave way to pessimism
- Jesus was popular with women
- Jesus was respected by men

- Jesus was joyful, and happy
- Jesus knew how to be angry, without losing His temper
- Jesus had peace

- Jesus was free of anxiety
- Jesus moved in great spiritual power: healing, deliverance, and miracles
- Jesus was free of low self-esteem
- Jesus wasn't addicted to food, alcohol, drugs, or sex
- Jesus was free of fear

- Jesus was free of the stranglehold of greed and materialism
- Jesus didn't rush around under pressure
- Jesus was free from bitterness

- Jesus was loved by kids
- Jesus wasn't irritable and impatient
- Jesus didn't live a futile life
- Jesus didn't yearn for power or fame
- Jesus had self-control, yet was free to enjoy himself
- Jesus didn't feel full of shame
- Jesus wasn't lazy
- Jesus never said the wrong thing
- Jesus knew how to rest

- Jesus never did things simply to please men
- Jesus was good at decision-making
- Jesus was equally at home with all levels of society
- Jesus was free of self-pity

- Jesus had many friends

- Jesus had nothing to hide
- Jesus could handle rejection

- Jesus was happy and positive to be around

- Jesus wasn't selfish
- Jesus wasn't despairing

- Jesus was radical
- Jesus was loving all the time
- Jesus never hid from the truth, he always lived in it
- Jesus didn't panic
- Jesus knew how to work
- Jesus knew how to handle money
- Jesus was holy, but never aloof from people
- Jesus was never unable to cope
- Jesus was completely secure in His Father's love
- Jesus was victorious over temptation and the devil
- Jesus was spontaneous and creative
- Jesus wasn't afraid of people
- Jesus could handle change
- Jesus was full of faith and hope
- Jesus changed everyone He met

Does this sound attractive? It's merely a glimpse of the life to the full that Jesus lived! It's the fullness of life that He intends us, His disciples, to have! It's a life that makes us radically contagious.

I have a vision, and it's this: that to our organisational

strength, we would add relational richness; that we would reach beyond good meetings, to grasp for community; that to efficient church structures we would add contagious, dangerous disciples. And that's what I've tried to explore in this book.

I've sought to include practical tools where possible, mainly to challenge our tendency to talk so much about 'what' and so little about 'how'. In doing so I recognise the risk that some may take the ideas in this book and try to apply them as some sort of formula. We seem quite prone to this, always reaching out for the new thing in the hope that it will be an off-the-peg 'answer'. I suspect in doing so we betray the shallowness of our motives. I can only hope that what I've written will be used in the way I intended: as a provocation to re-evaluating everything we do, and as a tool kit, discarding whatever is not useful or relevant to you.

I'm conscious that some of what I've said may be controversial. Where you disagree, I hope you will at least have found the discussion has provoked your thinking in some way. My intention is always to stimulate, not purposely to offend. I recognise that much of what I've expressed is, for me, work in progress. My hope is that in the coming years we will all learn so much from the Lord, and see the UK Church so transformed that much of what I've written will seem primitive and out of date.

My heart cry is to see our churches full of disciples, who are so full of life, that we will see the fulfilment of Zechariah's prophecy:

This is what the LORD Almighty says: 'In those days ten men from all languages and nations will take firm hold of one Jew by the hem of his robe and say, "Let us go with you, because we have heard that God is with you"' (Zech 8:23).

Appendix

GETTING THE MESSAGE ACROSS

The Scriptures encourage us to 'Be prepared to give an account of our hope (1 Peter 3:15) and to proclaim the message clearly' (Col 4:4). This isn't as straightforward as it may sound: I've argued earlier in this book that while holding fast to the centrality of the Cross, repentance and forgiveness, nevertheless we need to give much greater weight to the resurrection, the new life we have in Christ, the purposes that we're saved for, and to discipleship. The gospel presentation below is designed partly to help us think more clearly about the message we proclaim. It's also intended as a tool that may be of use when explaining this Gospel to not-yet-Christians. The diagram format renders it more accessible to people from a non-book culture or those for whom English is a second language.

The context

Sometimes our evangelism will take the form of a 'divine appointment' with a stranger. However, the instances of meeting someone we barely know and them asking 'What must I do to be saved?' are likely to be the exception. More usually it will be a process, centred on relationship building. Different aspects of the Gospel message will no doubt be discussed as the friendship develops. If we're thoroughly familiar with this presentation of the Gospel in diagram form, it's much easier to remember some of the key areas to introduce into our conversations. We need to be careful, though, to feed people only at the speed that they can chew! Nevertheless, in both instances there will come a point where it's appropriate to present the Gospel message showing how all the pieces fit together. This presentation is just one way of doing this. The more we're 'living the Gospel' by our love, words and actions, the easier it will be to explain what the Good News looks like in real life.

As a secondary point, a clear presentation of the Gospel can be very helpful to someone who has just become a Christian. People encounter God in a huge variety of ways, and even after having made a commitment to follow Christ they may have huge gaps in their understanding.

Diagrams i to xii show how the presentation works. This is followed by some notes of further explanation. Even if you're not drawn by the idea of a diagram, you may find some useful points in this section.

This presentation is based on a number of principles:

1. Gospel presentations often heavily emphasise the forgiveness of sins. While this is obviously an indispensable part of the good news, focussing on this *alone* creates several problems:

• it tells us what we're saved from, but not what we're saved for, leaving a rather lopsided, even negative slant;
• it tends to portray God as being there for man's sake, as his rescuer. In reality He's not there to meet our needs: we're here for His glory!
• because of the above point, it's easy to end up with a Gospel presentation that's man-centred instead of God-centred.

2. In a progressively post-Christian society, we often assume too much. In reality, most people have very little idea of what sin is, or why it's a problem relevant to them. We need to make sure our presentation of the Gospel helps people to understand these ideas, otherwise we'll be presenting a wonderful solution to a problem they don't know they have! This presentation talks instead about 'selfishness' and 'living to please ourselves', which are more readily understood than the word 'sin'. 'Changing' and 'turning' are used in place of the word 'repentance'. Having said that, it's useful to introduce Christian words, provided that we've explained them, because new Christians will encounter them soon enough in the Bible and in church meetings.

3. Because of our eagerness to see people born again and added to our churches we tend to push people too quickly, so that they make commitments before they're really ready. When we do this there's a much greater risk that they won't stay very long: our converts fail to become disciples.

Similarly, our fear of putting people off has led us to under-emphasise the mechanics of living the Christian life. The result has been that many Christians remain shallow: they simply don't know the depth of our calling, or decide that maturing involves costs of which they weren't aware and didn't sign up for. The Gospel is a message of how to be reconciled to God so that we can live life to the full. But this fullness of life is the outcome of a radical change: living entirely for God, not ourselves. Fullness of life is about choosing to become like Him. Becoming like Him, casting off our old self-pleasing nature, is something that needs training, discipline and work. We need to emphasise that being a disciple means living God's way in every practical day-to-day aspect of our lives, not merely subscribing to a set of beliefs or attending church meetings. Correspondingly, we need to be clear on all the resources that God makes available to enable us to live as disciples, and the joy, satisfaction and fulfilment of living God's way! This presentation of the Gospel reflects these principles.

4. Although text is included with the diagram, any presentation of the Gospel clearly needs to be tailored to suit the people involved.

Ultimately, this approach to presenting the Gospel is merely a tool for a job. If it's not suitable for you or for your friend, use something more effective instead! Whatever tools we use, we need to remember that tools are all they are: ultimately, new birth is a work of the Holy Spirit.

GOSPEL PRESENTATION

G O D

It all starts with God, and it's all about Him! And it's all about relationships: in the end, they're the most important thing in our lives.

God is all powerful, right across the page! He's the creator of everything, and holds it all together. He's perfect. He is love! He's a person, not a mystic force, and He reveals himself. He is supremely happy, He celebrates! He is One, but He is also Father, Son and Holy Spirit, similar to the way that 'God' is one word made up of three letters. They have a fantastic relationship, each one committed to the other, a perfect family.

LIFE to the FULL!
Living God-centred

God made mankind to extend and be part of His family: happy, fulfilled, celebrating God and being celebrated by Him! His intention was that they would develop and mature becoming increasingly like Himself. God's purpose was that human beings would live to love Him, and live for Him. By choosing to live God-centred lives, obeying a perfect loving Father, people would be directly plugged into the source of life, like being powered by the mains! This would be the most exciting and fulfilling life that a human being could have! Life to the full!

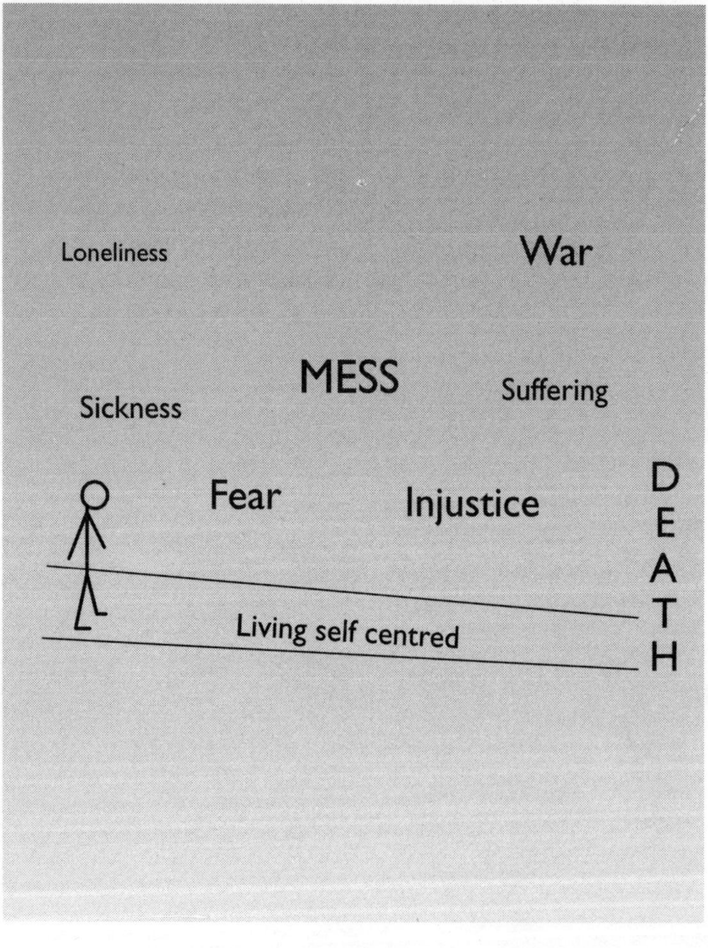
Loneliness
War
MESS
Suffering
Sickness
Fear
Injustice
DEATH
Living self centred

Sadly, although mankind was designed to live for God, people have chosen to turn away from Him. People live selfishly, doing things that offend and dishonour God. We can look around and see this everywhere, and if we're honest, 'self-centred' is a pretty good description of our lives too. Living like this has meant that we're separated from God. There's been a knock-on effect on creation too: while it's still very beautiful, we see disease, drought and other disasters. Everything's out of kilter. We're living in a grey twilight world, cut off from our relationship with God and we're cut off from our purpose. We're also cut off from the mains supply of life: it's as though we're running on batteries, which is why, when they run down, we face death. We're cut off from the person of God, the purposes of God and the power of God. Bad news!

What to do? Some people believe in God and see the need to be restored in relationship with Him, so they try to please God by being 'religious' or by doing lots of good deeds. The trouble is, no amount of human effort can bridge the huge gap back to God himself? In fact, every one of our selfish acts disqualifies us from being with Him. More than that, it's not just what we do, but our selfish hearts that need to change. Other people know deep down that they have a purpose, but being cut off from it, try to find a substitute: they pursue power, money, sex, or a 'cause' of some sort. But it doesn't work. Many people, cut-off from God's perfect love, find refuge from the pain of life in drugs, crime, alcohol, and so on. Quite often people sense the need to belong to God's family, so they look for substitutes: this leads to the 'us and them' attitude that's behind nationalism, racism, etc. All of these are roads that come to a dead end. Life without God really is a mess! The key point is this: nothing we could possibly do is able to bridge that gap back to God! In fact, God says that the only way to cancel out the selfish things we've done, and to be free of the hold that selfishness has on our hearts is for us to die. We're in trouble!

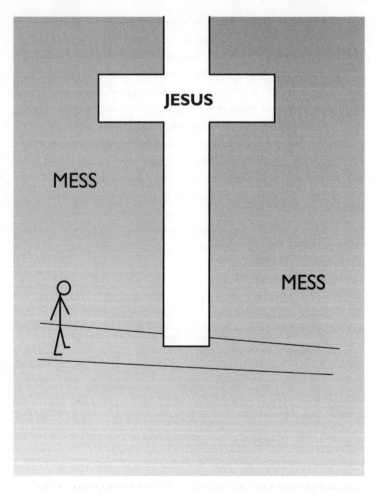

Here's some good news! What we couldn't do, God did — He mounted a rescue! He chose to come to the earth, as Jesus Christ, from heaven, right into the mess we've made! He lived as a perfect human being, showing us our potential, what we're made for! He was crucified and experienced death, but in doing so, He died in our place, as a substitute. If you like, He paid the death penalty that we faced for all the things we've done in our lives that dishonour God. He cancelled out all those selfish acts that separate us from God. He proved that He was more powerful than death by rising from the grave, and then He returned to the Father in heaven. In effect, He's created a bridge across the gap, so that we can have a restored relationship with God, and get back to our original purpose: life to the full with God!

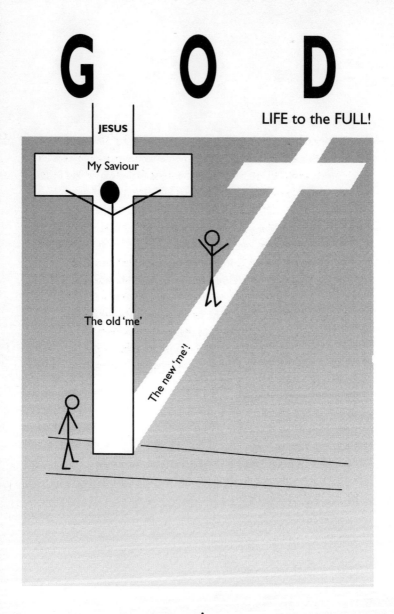

vi

Although Jesus died on the Cross nearly 2000 years ago, He created a way back to God that is still open to us today. So, here we are: everyone on the planet has a big decision to make. We can ignore Jesus, and carry right on with our lives as before. Or we can rely on Jesus as our rescuer. If we do this, we're accepting that Jesus died in our place. This means that we're forgiven for all the selfish things we've ever done. In a sense, through Jesus, we too died on the Cross, so the stranglehold that selfishness had over us is broken: we're free to live a new way! Just as we died with Jesus on the cross, so also we've been given a new life through Jesus rising from the dead. This is why Christians sometimes talk about being 'born-again' into a new life. This is what it means to know Jesus as our Saviour. But there's more: it's not just what we've been saved FROM that we need to understand, but what we're saved FOR . . .

G O D

LIFE to the FULL!

Jesus: My Lord

The new 'me'!

We're saved so that we can live as we're meant to live, to get back on track of our original purpose. In short, living a life that's God-centred, loving him and living His way. This is living the 'Way of the Cross'. It's how we live life to the full. This is what we mean by acknowledging Jesus as our Lord. Becoming a Christian means that you've chosen to accept Jesus both as Saviour AND Lord.

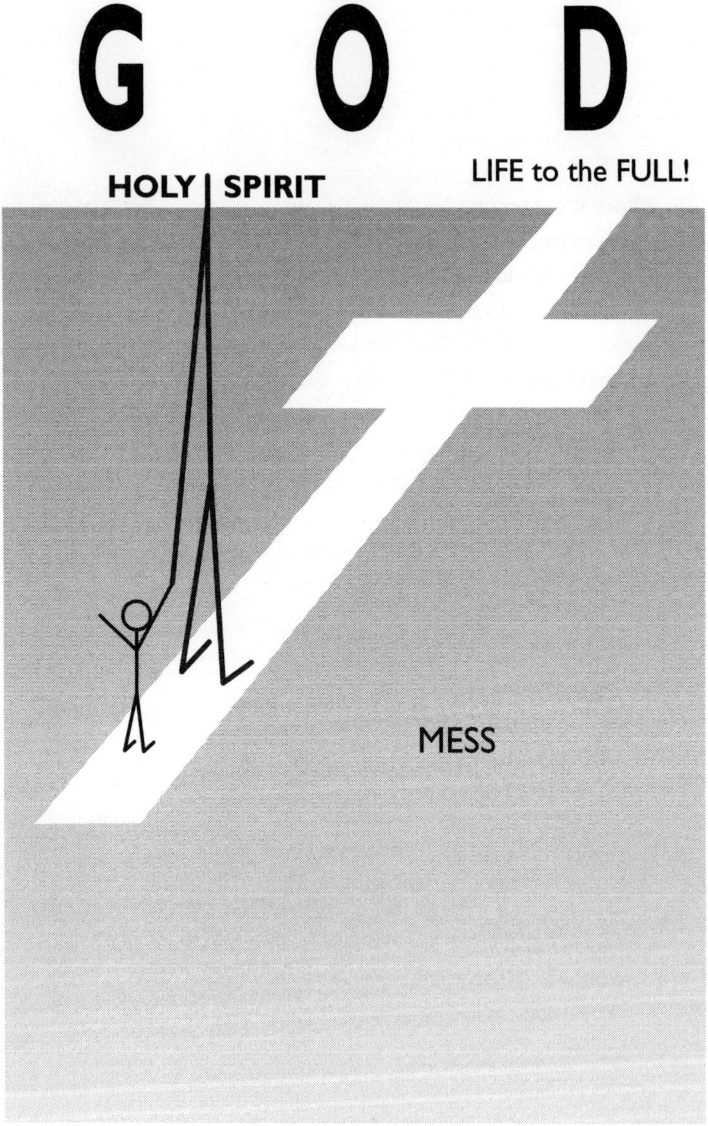
GOD
HOLY SPIRIT
LIFE to the FULL!
MESS

Living this new God-centred life, and becoming increasingly like Him, is called discipleship. It's not easy. It's true that our old life, which was in the grip of selfishness, died on the Cross. But there are still many of the old ways of thinking and behaving that are ingrained. It's a bit like a butterfly hatching from its cocoon. It's already been transformed from its life as a caterpillar, but still needs to struggle out of the dead shell to be able to fly properly. So how can we do this? It's certainly a challenge, but God has given us all the resources we need. Most importantly, He's given us his Holy Spirit. This means that God himself is living within us! The Holy Spirit changes us, making us increasingly like Him, and He gives us all the power we need to do things God's way: we're plugged into the mains now! So, yes, there is a cost to being a disciple, that we need to think carefully about. If we're putting God first, we're no longer putting ourselves first! On the other hand, we need to think about the cost of not being a disciple: we miss out on eternal life, true freedom, real joy, peace!

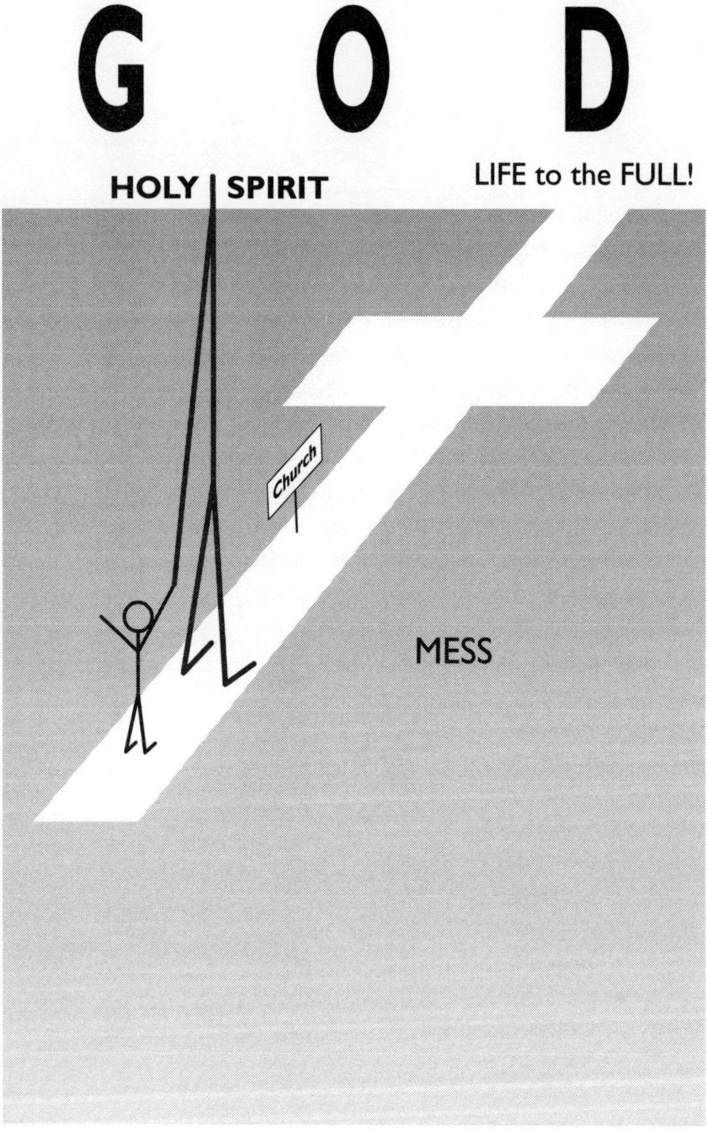
G O D
HOLY SPIRIT
LIFE to the FULL!
Church
MESS

Although we have the Holy Spirit within us, living God's way and becoming more like Him isn't purely automatic: we can't just sit back, we need to learn to work in partnership with the Holy Spirit to get free of all of our old lifestyle. And we're still living in a world that's a mess, so becoming a Christian doesn't make life all plain sailing! But God is with us in the tough times, and will even use them to help us grow. God also helps us by putting us together with other Christians: church. Our new life is designed to be lived this way, we're not meant to go it alone. The purpose of church is to help us know God better, and become more like Him. But it's also to make God known. We become part of a radical community of people whose lifestyle and relationships show the world the good news about God's love.

The Choice

If we choose not to follow Jesus, our future isn't promising. But as Christians we're getting bigger, becoming all that we're meant to be! It's true that our bodies will age and die, but we don't need to fear death any more. God will give us a new body that never wears out! And in the end, God has promised that He will come and create a new earth for His family, where there'll be no more pain, sickness, suffering or death. We'll be with God forever, living lives full of joy and adventure!

Do something about it!

How do I become a Christian?
Basically, there's some decisions to make: read through this sheet first! When you are ready to make those decisions, there are some things to say to God (praying) and some actions to take.

Praying
Lord, I admit that I've done things that offend you. In particular
....

I admit that I've lived my life to please myself or other people instead of you. Because of all this I'm cut off from you.

I realise that I can't cancel out these wrong things I've done, or change my own heart attitude, but today I'm making a choice to turn away from them and turn towards you, asking you to rescue me.

I choose to acknowledge you, Jesus, as my Saviour. Thank you that you died in my place, paying the penalty for everything wrong I've ever done, or will do. Thank you Jesus, for this gift, that I'm free from any need to feel guilty before you.

Thank you that my old life died with you on that Cross: the hold that living to please myself had over me is broken! Thank you for the new life you've given me, that I'm born again!

I choose to acknowledge you Jesus, as my Lord: instead of living to please myself, I'm choosing now to live to please You. Thank you for giving me your Holy Spirit to help me break free of old selfish ways of thinking and behaving, and to teach me how to live life to the full. Please fill me to overflowing with your Holy Spirit!

Thank you that you have forgiven me and given me eternal life. Thank you that you've welcomed me home as your son/daughter.

Action

Talk through with an experienced Christian ways in which you can put right things you've done which dishonour God. Is there something you need to give back, someone to say sorry to, someone to forgive?

Tell people you know that you've become a Christian. Chat the good news: everyone needs to hear it!

Ask your Christian friend how to become involved in a Church, so that you can meet others members of your new family, and learn together. Many Churches have small groups that meet in people's homes and these are good places to start.

Ask your Christian friend to explain about baptism, and arrange for you to be baptised.

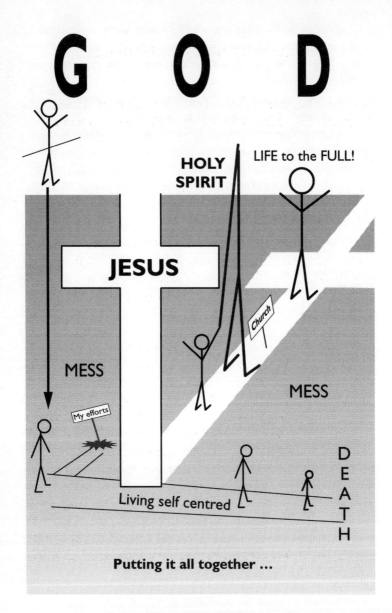

Explanatory notes to the diagram

These are explanatory notes on each stage of drawing the diagram, which expand on the text included on each page.

Diagram i

The purpose of this first stage of the diagram is to put the focus on God right away. There may be a number of different attributes you'd like to talk about with your friend, perhaps relating to previous conversations you've had with them about God. It's important to make sure you include His power, His perfection, and His love, being key elements later on. It can be helpful to refer to God as Creator because for many people this is a familiar idea, even if many people simultaneously accept evolution theory.

This is also a good time to challenge popular misconceptions in our culture: firstly, by affirming that God is a person, not a mystic force. This 'mystic force' idea has been strengthened by the influence of Eastern religions. It's vital that our friend understands that God is a person so that the idea of a relationship with God has meaning. Secondly, it's very helpful to talk about God's happiness: this comes as an interesting surprise to most people, and challenges the misconception that 'God stuff' may be worthy, even necessary, but certainly boring. The Scriptures refer to Jesus as 'full of joy through the Holy Spirit' (Luke 10:21) and to the 'blessed (happy) God' (1 Tim 1:11, 1 Tim 6:15). It's a sad comment on the Church in our country that in general people have not seen the likeness of God's joy reflected in His people.

Diagram ii

The main aim at this stage of the diagram is to explain God's purpose in creating mankind, His ultimate purposes. It's tempting to talk about Adam and Eve in the Garden of Eden. But we need to face the fact that the idea of evolution is so embedded in our society that many find it difficult to relate to the Genesis account, and it can make our message seem quaint, and backward looking. It can also seriously side-track the conversation. The Scriptures are clear that Genesis shows God's plans as they start, not at their climax. God's intention from before the beginning of time was that we would be 'conformed to the likeness of His Son' (Rom 8:29), that we would be in union with Him ('Christ in us, the hope of glory' Col 1:27), that we would know Him fully, and rule with Him. Our destination is perfect fulfilment, pure happiness, true freedom, lasting for all eternity!

This may not be easy for a not-yet-Christian mind to grasp, especially because our society has conditioned us to be suspicious when something sounds so attractive. Also, the message that humans are designed to live in obedience to God, and are therefore perfectly fulfilled in doing so is a radically counter-cultural message. We need to find ways of communicating this truth in ways that are relevant to our friend, and as specific as possible. One starting point would be to say what we personally are most looking forward to. Alternatively, our previous conversations with our not-yet-Christian friend may have given us an idea of what they are primarily looking for in life. The more clearly we portray 'life to the full', the more powerful will be the contrast when we go on to describe the world as it currently is, and our choice to 'live for self'. We need to help people to see this contrast, the horror of a fallen world, of our personal separation from God: it's so familiar that most people regard it as both normal and without alternative.

Understanding God's purposes gives us a broader perspective. Instead of seeing redemption as an end in itself, we begin to see it in its exciting context: God's way of putting us back on the pathway to our ultimate destiny. If redemption alone fills our whole vision we can easily become man-centred. It also becomes harder to make sense of discipleship, which can easily be seen as an add-on. A fuller understanding of what we are saved *for* quickly establishes the absolute necessity of discipleship.

Diagram iii

Here we draw a sharp contrast between humanity as intended, and fallen humanity in a fallen world. By talking about death, something everyone faces, and the impact of the Fall on nature, we're helping to convey the scale of the Gospel message. This challenges the misconception that the Gospel message is somehow relevant only to our 'spiritual side', or limited to our moral behaviour. The Gospel is not only relevant, but in fact central to everything.

Our main aim, of course, is to help our friend see that they personally need rescuing. It's better to use the phrases 'living to please ourselves' and 'selfishness' rather than talk about 'sin'. One reason for this is that most people in our culture regard sin as an archaic term, which can make us sound old fashioned. But more importantly, many people simply wouldn't regard themselves as living sinfully. In their eyes sin is perceived as robbing banks, or mugging old ladies. On this basis they feel they've lived a decent enough life, and are probably 'doing OK with God'. It's a commonly held view that God is satisfied if we've done more good than bad in our lives, as judged, conveniently, by oneself. By contrast, asked whether they live to please God or live to please themselves, most people would (perhaps grudgingly) acknowledge their selfish motivation. Contrasting life and death, connection to the mains with running on batteries, may start to open eyes to the need for salvation.

Diagram iv

The main purpose here is to help our not-yet-Christian friend realise that they're struggling with a life which is cut off from God, and that there's absolutely no hope of remedy by their own efforts. We might not need to draw and explain all the arrows: it may make sense to focus on those issues that are most relevant to our friend. On the other hand, drawing all the arrows communicates that the Gospel provides powerful insights into the way that everybody behaves. This emphasises both the direct relevance and broad scope of the Gospel message. It's part of the process of establishing credibility.

Concluding with a statement that God has declared our death to be the only solution is important. It's a reminder that God has the authority; it emphasises the seriousness of living away from God; it reinforces the idea of our helplessness. It also lays a foundation for understanding that God's solution is going to be wonderful news, but also that we should expect it to involve a radical impact on our life.

Diagram v

This stage of the diagram focuses directly on Jesus: His incarnation, life, death, resurrection, and ascension. The aim is to show that the Gospel is God's initiative; that Jesus is the perfect model for living; that His death is the solution to our separation from God; that His resurrection and ascension offer us new life.

Diagram vi

At this stage of the diagram, we're aiming to show that what happened 2,000 years ago is totally relevant now. From talking about the Gospel in general terms, we shift to the specific: everyone faces a personal challenge about the direction they choose to take. It's important to communicate the principle that our old life has been crucified. Knowing that the *power* of selfishness in us is broken is a vital resource when as disciples we stand against the *presence* of selfishness in our lives.

Diagram vii

If we've communicated our intended purpose as human beings effectively, presenting the Lordship of Christ will seem an obvious and natural part of being restored to this purpose. It's vital that we recognise Lordship, what we're saved *for*, as integral to the process of becoming a Christian. While it's true that we become more submitted as we mature, it's vital that Lordship is never perceived as an optional extra.

Diagram viii

Sadly, discipleship, the process of becoming more like Jesus through obedience to Him, is poorly understood by many Christians. It often seems to be portrayed as the price we pay for our salvation, something we're stuck with because we've been saved, the small print at the bottom of the Gospel message. It's also common to think of discipleship in terms of the debt we owe to Jesus for saving us. The idea is that since God loves us and died for us now we owe him everything; our debt to Him is such that the least we can do is to obey Him. This type of thinking is surprisingly widespread and has even found its way into worship choruses and songs.

But it's not biblical. The message of the Gospel is that Jesus came to pay our debts, not create them! In practical terms, seeking to obey God on the basis of obligation or debt paying soon becomes unsustainable. Our new life, born of the seed of God, eagerly desires to obey God, purely from love. Discipleship is the tremendously exciting process of shedding the dross of our old life, learning to obey, growing in maturity.

It's about developing an ever-greater likeness to our heavenly Dad, and moving increasingly into the life for which God intended, a life of complete joy and fulfilment! Yes, there is a cost in this, and hard work, and Jesus himself reminded us of the importance of counting the cost before we build the tower. But equally we need to be aware of the wonderful fruit of discipleship. And the cost of choosing not to follow Him. New Christians are easier to disciple and less likely to backslide if they are given the full picture before making their decision.

This is where we also introduce the Holy Spirit. It's vital for a new Christian to understand the awesome truth of having God dwelling within us, and the power this gives us for living His way!

Diagram ix

This diagram focuses on three issues.

1. Work

We need to emphasise this point: discipleship involves hard work! *Epidemic of Life* tackles two misconceptions. Firstly, that we need merely to 'let go and let God', in order to change: this way of thinking amounts to opting out of the responsibility that we have for our growth as disciples. It's really a spiritual-sounding justification for being lazy and comfortable. Secondly, the misconception that struggle equals legalism. By contrast, the Scriptures call us to 'take hold' (Phil 3:12; 1 Tim 6:12,19). Paul calls the Philippians to 'work out their salvation with fear and trembling' (2:12). He frequently describes the Christian life as a race to be run. The writer to the Hebrews defines the mature as those 'who by *constant practice* have *trained* themselves to distinguish good from evil' (5:14). It is perfectly true that we must rely on the Holy Spirit's enabling for all that we do, but the choice remains our responsibility. Importantly, even when we are making the right choices and relying on the power of the Holy Spirit, we will still experience struggles, still need to work hard. Paul specifically says to the Colossians 'To this end I labour, struggling with all his energy, which so powerfully works in me' (1:29).

What form does this hard work take? Firstly, it involves the shedding of our old way of life. This means training our will through constant practice to choose God's way rather than ours, all the time relying on the Holy Spirit to empower our choice. It means breaking old habits, old patterns of behaviour, taking thoughts captive, submitting our bodies. The means are essentially the same: our choices, empowered by the Holy Spirit.

Secondly, discipleship involves hard work in learning to obey God. In the Great Commission Jesus specifically said that disciples would need to be taught to obey. This will mean challenging laziness, fear, and the desire to do our own thing. A large proportion of the New Testament is given over to instruction on how to live God's way: principles relating to what we say; instructions for our relationships (with the opposite sex, children, masters, servants, leaders, followers, rich and poor); the way we handle our money and possessions, and so on. Reorientating every aspect of our lives is a challenge. Again, the pattern is the same: our willingness, coupled to God's enabling.

Spiritual disciplines. This is covered more thoroughly in Chapter 5 of *Epidemic of Life*. In summary, spiritual disciplines are means, not ends. They train us to challenge our self-centredness, and nurture our new nature. Jesus and the Apostles trained in this way.

The joy of discipleship. In emphasising that discipleship involves work, it's crucial to see this in a positive light. God instituted work before the Fall, so it has always been part of His plan for us. Discipleship's work is in putting off the old nature so that we can live in the new; it's throwing off the old yoke so that we can wear Jesus' easy yoke. As we work at discipleship, the purpose and result is that we move increasingly into the happiness, freedom and power that characterised Jesus himself.

2. No 'opt-out' on troubles

We need to deal clearly with a popular misconception, by stating that bad things happen to Christians as they do to anybody else. But the difference is that we can have an entirely different perspective on them when we know that God is Sovereign, and that He is with us.

3. Church

Our society is highly individualistic, and it's a common thought (even amongst some Christians) that you don't have to go to church to be a Christian. Actually, it's a sad reflection, that even where people have a measure of respect for Christianity (as they understand it) they generally have a poor opinion of the Church. This makes it tempting to present the Gospel purely in terms of establishing an individual relationship with God, leaving 'church' to the small print. But the Bible doesn't give us this option.

The Scriptures are clear that when we become a Christian we become part of a family. It's essential that we meet together with our family (Heb 10:25). Church is our training ground where we receive teaching, opportunities to serve, and the challenge of building loving relationships with people that are flawed, as we are, and different from us in character, temperament and culture. Church is where we discover that although we're unique, we're designed by God to be joined to others as members of Christ's body. Opting out of this deprives other people of what we could bring to them, and means that we miss the opportunity to be fully the person God intended us to be. When we take the risk of belonging, of making commitment to others, we begin to discover the corporate dimension to activities such as prayer and worship. Finally, it's as a family that we can resource each other in our call to be salt and light to the world.

Belonging, commitment, being willing to make some personal sacrifices for the benefit of the whole, are ideas that are challenging to our culture. Even within the Church we all know of numbers of immature Christians, especially in urban areas, who go from church to church searching for spiritual excitement, looking to take rather than to give, moving on to more comfortable places when difficulties and challenges arise. Sadly, such shallow roots stunt growth into maturity.

For all these reasons we need to be clear from the outset about the central place of 'church' in the life of a disciple. You may want to refer in general terms to the commitments that new members make to your own church.

Diagram x

This page of the diagram aims to clarify the choice, the need to make a decision. However it also puts this choice into the context of our future hope. At a personal level it's good to emphasise life beyond death. At a general level, it's important to convey the idea that God is going to deal with all the mess that we see in this fallen world. The Gospel is not merely a life raft from a sinking ship. It's about an advancing Kingdom that will eventually engulf the mess: God is big enough to make everything right!

Obviously it's only possible to outline these points briefly during a presentation of the Gospel.

Diagram xi

Time to think

After presenting the Gospel using the diagram, your friend may be eager to respond and ready to become a Christian, using a pattern along the lines of diagram xi. On the other hand, don't be afraid to give them more time to digest: after all you've communicated some weighty material, some of which is probably new to them.

There can be a temptation to try and press for a 'decision' on the spot, based on a fear of losing the initiative. But major decisions involving death and life need time, and a hasty response is more likely to be followed by 'second thoughts'. It may be better to make a date specifically to talk further, perhaps in a day or two, so as not to lose momentum, and while what you've said is still fresh in their mind. Our fear of losing the opportunity is probably exaggerated if we have an established friendship. And we need to remember that God is drawing people to Himself.

Real repentance

On the whole, the Church in this country has tended to emphasise salvation in terms of what we're saved from (cancelling of our sins), and given too little priority to what we're saved for: transformation into His likeness. This has led to an unhealthy telescoping of the process of repentance.

For people wanting to be born again a simple general prayer asking for forgiveness of sins is often deemed to suffice. Likewise many Christians have relegated repentance to a brief non-specific confession of sins followed by a headlong rush into asking to be forgiven. We've produced a mentality of 'fast-fix' forgiveness. One result is that we see Christians going through this process for exactly the same sins over and over again, with little apparent change or growth.

The Scriptures present a different picture. The word we translate as repentance, *metanoia*, itself means a 'change of mind or purpose'. This isn't a superficial acknowledgement of errors that need to be wiped clean, it's a considered decision to change. The Bible says that there should be fruits of repentance. This has a forward-looking dimension in terms of a change of behaviour, and a retrospective element through making restora-

APPENDIX 197

tion. When Zaccheus repented, specific action followed, including the reimbursement of people he had cheated (Luke 19).

We need to recover the biblical model for repentance. This means being willing to face our sins squarely, asking God to reveal them to us, specifically. We need to give time to understanding how offensive they are to God, how damaging to us, and to other people, and to confess accordingly. It's when we have done this that we begin to appreciate our forgiveness more genuinely; and we understand more clearly both *why* we need to change and our complete dependence on the Holy Spirit to do so.

Repentance of this mettle seems to have characterised not only the early Christians but also revivals throughout history. No doubt the evidence of changed lives and acts of restitution will prove to be equally effective witnesses in our times.

Diagram xii

Simply a summary of the diagram, to show how all the parts fit together.

NOTES

Chapter 2. Firing on all Cylinders

1. The concept of the happiness of God has been explored brilliantly in *The Pleasures of God* by John Piper (Multnomah Press, 1991, ISBN 0-88070-537-X).
2. Many of the ideas in this chapter are more fully explored in *Ultimate Intention* by DeVern Fromke (Sure Foundation, 2522 Colony Court, Indianapolis, IN 46280, USA. First published 1963, revised edition 1998, ISBN 0 936595 02 7).

Chapter 3. How Change Works

John Piper's exciting book *Future Grace* (Inter-Varsity Press, 1998, ISBN 0 85111 162 9) explores this whole area in much more depth.

Chapter 4. Tools for Transformation

1. Ralph Neighbour sets out his cell vision in *Where do we go from here?* (Touch Publications Inc., ISBN 1 880828 54 5). Ralph Neighbour's cell church materials can be obtained in the UK through YWAM: Eileen Jackson, Kings Lodge, Watling St, Nuneaton, CV10 OTZ. Tel: 01203 348128.

2. A short while ago I attended a training course run by IGNIS, a Christian counselling organisation based in Germany. Their work in this whole area is very exciting and certainly groundbreaking. IGNIS was founded by two German professional psychotherapists who became Christians. They initially attempted to integrate biblical insights into their existing models. God had other ideas! He prompted them to start afresh, using the biblical principles to develop completely different models. Their approach is distinctive both in the degree to which it sees ordinary members of the local church as the key players in the process of personal change, and in the dependence on the Holy Spirit's guidance. They can be contacted at the following address:

IGNIS-Academy for Christian Psychology
Kanzler-Stuertzel-Str.2
D-97318 Kitzingen
Tel: 9321 133 040
Fax: 9321 133 041

Chapter 5. Spiritual Fitness

1. I have found the following books outstandingly helpful in this area:
Richard Foster, *Prayer* (Hodder and Stoughton, 1992, ISBN 0 340 56900 X).
Richard Foster, *Celebration of Discipline* (Hodder and Stoughton, 1980, ISBN 0 340 50007 7).
Gordon MacDonald, *Ordering Your Private World* (Highland Books, 1984, ISBN 0 946616 31 0).
Richard Foster and James Byron Smith, eds., *Devotional Classics* (Hodder and Stoughton, 1993, ISBN 0 340 60121 3).
Dallas Willard, *The Spirit of the Disciplines* (Hodder and Stoughton, 1996, ISBN 0 340 66513 0).

William Dalrymple, *From the Holy Mountain* (Flamingo, 1998, ISBN 0 00 654774 5).

2. Dalrymple, *From the Holy Mountain*, pp 409–10.

Chapter 6. Be Filled!

1. CS Lewis, *The Screwtape Letters* (Fount, 1998, ISBN 0 00628 060 9), Letter IV.   '

Chapter 8. Learning Keys

1. These issues are explored much more extensively in David Oliver's highly stimulating book, *Work: Prison or Place of Destiny?* (Word Publishing, 1999, ISBN 1-8602-4340-1).

2. Quoted with permission from *Booked Out* by Chris Key, Don Smith, Jenny Richardson and Roy Dorey, (CPAS, 1995, ISBN 1 8976 6024 3). CPAS can be contacted at Athena Drive, Tachbrook Park, Warwick, CV34 6NG.

3. UNLOCK can be contacted at 336a City Road, Sheffield S2 1GA. Tel. 0114-276-2038.

4. The 'Y' course is a joint project of the Y Foundation, Word Publishing, Agapé and CPAS. Further information can be obtained from Word Publishing Tel: 01908 364206.

5. The implications of new technology are explored much more fully in *Cyberchurch* by Patrick Dixon, (Kingsway, 1998, ISBN 0 85476 711 8).

Chapter 9. A Local Church Strategy for Developing Contagious Christians

1. A similar approach has been developed by Rick Warren in the Saddleback Church, and is described more fully in his excellent book *The Purpose Driven Church*, (Zondervan, 1995, ISBN 0-310-20106-3).

2. Warren, *The Purpose Driven Church.*
3. I highly recommend the 'Workshop' course. While a significant proportion of course members are from charismatic evangelical churches, the course leaders represent a diversity of backgrounds including Mennonite and Anabaptist. As a result, the course is particularly effective at challenging established theology in a way that provokes people to think for themselves and throw off their blinkers. The course has many practical elements as well as intellectual, and can be followed at different levels, from no assessment, up to 'A'-level standard. The course runs for one weekend per month over 11 months and is based at five centres around the UK. This makes the course ideal for those who wish to stretch themselves, but who are unable to take time off for full time study due to family, career or other reasons. Prospectuses can be obtained from: Workshop Central Office, 104 Townend Lane, Deepcar, Sheffield, S36 2TS. Tel: 0114 288 8816.
4. Warren, *The Purpose Driven Church.*

Chapter 10. '. . . And Forceful Men . . .'

The 'Promise Keepers' is a 'Christ-centred ministry dedicated to uniting men through vital relationships, to become godly influences in their world'. Promise Keepers began in the early 1990's in the USA, and in 1996 over a million men met in 22 stadium and arena events. The seven promises of a Promise Keeper are:

i. A Promise Keeper is committed to honouring Jesus Christ through worship, prayer and obedience to God's Word in the power of the Holy Spirit.
ii. A Promise Keeper is committed to pursuing vital relationships with a few other men, understanding that he needs brothers to help him keep his promises.

iii. A Promise Keeper is committed to practising spiritual, moral, ethical, and sexual purity.

iv. A Promise Keeper is committed to building strong marriages and families through love, protection and biblical values.

v. A Promise Keeper is committed to supporting the mission of his church by honouring and praying for his pastor, and by actively giving his time and resources.

vi. A Promise Keeper is committed to reaching beyond any racial and denominational barriers to demonstrate the power of biblical unity.

vii. A Promise Keeper is committed to influencing his world, being obedient to the Great Commandment (see Mark 12:30–30) and the Great Commission (see Matthew 28:19–20).

The above information was drawn from the Promise Keepers' web site: http://www.promisekeepers.org

Chapter 12. Contagious Evangelism

1. Many of the points raised here are explored in much greater depth in Pete Gilbert's excellent book *Radical Evangelism: A New Look at an Old Commission*, (Word (UK) Ltd./Pioneer 1992, ISBN 0-85009-728-2).

2. *Sowing, Reaping, Keeping* by Laurence Singlehurst, (Crossways Books, first edition 1995, reprinted 1996, 1997, ISBN 1-85684-052-2).

3. *'The mass of men lead lives of quiet desperation.'* Henry David Thoreau